Formal Recognition of Employer-Sponsored Instruction:
Conflict and Collegiality in Postsecondary Education

by Nancy S. Nash and Elizabeth M. Hawthorne

ASHE-ERIC Higher Education Report No. 3, 1987

Prepared by

 *Clearinghouse on Higher Education*
The George Washington University

Published by

 *Association for the Study of*
Higher Education

Jonathan D. Fife,
Series Editor

Cite as

Nash, Nancy S., and Hawthorne, Elizabeth M. *Formal Recognition of Employer-Sponsored Instruction: Conflict and Collegiality in Postsecondary Education*. ASHE-ERIC Higher Education Report No. 3. Washington, D.C.: Association for the Study of Higher Education, 1987.

Managing Editor: Christopher Rigaux
Manuscript Editor: Barbara M. Fishel/Editech

The ERIC Clearinghouse on Higher Education invites individuals to submit proposals for writing monographs for the Higher Education Report series. Proposals must include:
1. A detailed manuscript proposal of not more than five pages.
2. A chapter-by-chapter outline.
3. A 75-word summary to be used by several review committees for the initial screening and rating of each proposal.
4. A vita.
5. A writing sample.

Library of Congress Catalog Card Number 87-71299
ISSN 0884-0040
ISBN 0-913317-37-3

Cover design by Michael David Brown, Rockville, Maryland

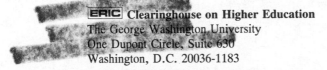

ERIC Clearinghouse on Higher Education
The George Washington University
One Dupont Circle, Suite 630
Washington, D.C. 20036-1183

ASHE **Association for the Study of Higher Education**
Texas A&M University
Department of Educational Administration
Harrington Education Center
College Station, Texas 77843

Office of Educational
Research and Improvement
U.S. Department of Education

This publication was prepared partially with funding from the Office of Educational Research and Improvement, U.S. Department of Education, under contract no. 400-86-0017. The opinions expressed in this report do not necessarily reflect the positions or policies of OERI or the Department.

EXECUTIVE SUMMARY

What Is Corporate Education?
This report discusses the extensive education and training
programs established and run by corporations and other organizations, largely profit-making enterprises whose primary purpose is something other than education, in the context of traditional higher education. As used in this report, "corporate education" is education offered by a business or industry for
its own employees.

How Extensive Is Corporate Education?
Corporate education is an extensive, multifaceted endeavor,
costing billions of dollars, educating millions of people, and
absorbing many working hours annually.

It is estimated, for example, that approximately $30 billion
to $50 billion is spent on formal employee education and $180
billion on informal, on-the-job education. Employees in companies with 500 or more employees—4.4 million people—can expect to receive frequent instruction paid for and provided
by their employers.

Is Corporate Education a Threat to Higher Education?
As colleges and universities strive to respond to the needs of
nontraditional students, they often find that corporate educators
have preceded them. Corporations, with the assistance of the
American Council on Education (ACE) and the New York Regents, have had their courses evaluated, frequently leading to
the granting of credit for corporate coursework by colleges and
universities.

Courses offered by corporations range from remedial to
postgraduate-level management and technical courses. Corporations have even founded their own colleges, known as "corporate colleges." These educational efforts potentially could
threaten the health, and devalue the worth, of higher education,
but in fact, corporate education is compatible with—indeed
complements—traditional higher education.

Higher education in the United States has been responsive to
the needs of the workplace since the beginning of the federal
period. The prevailing dialogue in higher education has long
been the weighing of tradeoffs—practically and philosophi-
cally—between general education and what now is called
"career education."

The formal recognition of instruction independent of the
providers is a multifaceted and complex enterprise on the post-

secondary education scene in and of itself. These efforts have accomplished two things. First, the structural conformity of noncollegiate instruction with collegiate instruction (for example, associating credit hours with contact hours) facilitates transfers and students' mobility and opens up an array of potential cooperative efforts between businesses and colleges. Second, they have served as a major channel of communication between school and corporation about educational content and methods. This report presents the interaction between corporate education and these recognition processes, a path by which noncollegiate education can wend its way into the most traditional patterns of higher education.

Innovations find their way into higher education in several ways, one of which is when external institutions appear on the scene to challenge, titillate, and/or draw attention to significant issues. The emergence of corporate education with its interest in formal recognition offers opportunities and challenges to higher education in the way it teaches, the students it seeks, and the perception of the purposes of education. The growth of corporate education is a stimulus to both internal collegiate debates and public policy decision making.

What Can Be Expected from the Proliferation Of Corporate Education?

Many profitable educational ventures have been initiated that were provoked by employers' recognition of their responsibility for developing their employees. The American University, for example, using its own faculty, offers a Master of Science in toxicology at Litton Industries, and the Massachusetts Institute of Technology cooperates in an education program with IBM and Digital Equipment. An indirect benefit to colleges resulting from an increased awareness of conditions in higher education on the part of business and industry has been the use of modern technology by colleges and universities to educate future employees. And a national discussion on the role of colleges and universities in American society has been stimulated by heightened awareness of shared national needs.

Corporate education is well established, a large enterprise, and increasingly more professional. The factors that led employers to begin to educate and train their employees continue to affect their choices as technology changes, as businesses create proprietary information to share with their employees, and as employees need to learn new skills or enhance current skills to make a contribution to the workplace. If traditional collegiate institutions and associations ignore or discount corporate education, they will do so at their own peril. There is room for accommodation and cooperation that will serve learners and their providers as well.

ADVISORY BOARD

CONSULTING EDITORS

Paul A. Albrecht
Executive Vice President and Dean
Claremont Graduate School

L. Leon Campbell
Provost and Vice President for Academic Affairs
University of Delaware

Judith A. Clementson-Mohr
Director of Psychological Services
Purdue University

Roderick S. French
Vice President for Academic Affairs
George Washington University

Timothy Gallineau
Vice President for Student Development
Saint Bonaventure University

Milton Greenberg
Provost
American University

James C. Hearn
Associate Professor, Educational Policy and Administration
University of Minnesota

Margaret Heim
Senior Research Officer
Teachers Insurance and Annuity Association/College
  Retirement Equity Fund

Hans H. Jenny
Executive Vice President
Chapman College

Jules B. LaPidus
President
Council of Graduate Schools in the United States

Judith B. McLaughlin
Research Associate on Education and Sociology
Harvard University

Theodore J. Marchese
Vice President
American Association for Higher Education

Arthur S. Marmaduke
Director
Eureka Project

John D. Marshall
Assistant to the Executive Vice President and Provost
Georgia State University

Sheila A. Murdick
Director, National Program on Noncollegiate-Sponsored
 Instruction
New York State Board of Regents

L. Jackson Newell
Professor and Dean
University of Utah

Steven G. Olswang
Assistant Provost for Academic Affairs
University of Washington

Thomas J. Quatroche
Professor and Chair, Educational Foundations Department
State University College at Buffalo

S. Andrew Schaffer
Vice President and General Counsel
New York University

John P. Sciacca
Assistant Professor, Health, Physical Education, and Recreation
Northern Arizona University

Henry A. Spille
Director, Office on Educational Credits and Credentials
American Council on Education

CONTENTS

FOREWORD

We first addressed the issue of corporate training programs in a 1984 report by Suzanne Morse, *Employee Educational Programs: Implications for Industry and Higher Education*. Because of the increased role of these training programs and the perceived increased threat to traditional higher education, we return to the topic here to examine the even more formal educational activities of corporations, in particular at the accredited degree-granting programs.

As emphasized by both Morse and Nash/Hawthorne, industry has been involved in training employees for a long time. Therefore, this is not a new phenomenon that needs to be addressed in light of how traditional higher education is serving society. Certain questions must be kept in mind during the reading of the report: (1) Has traditional higher education failed in its educational responsibilities? (2) Conversely, should traditional higher education be involved in many of these corporate areas? (3) Or, from a more middle ground, how can traditional higher education and corporate education cooperate to make the best use of each of their strengths?

This report, written by Nancy Nash, director of personnel and planning at the University of Wisconsin–Superior, and Elizabeth Hawthorne, assistant professor of higher education at the University of Toledo, tracks the extent to which employer-sponsored education programs have penetrated the traditional domain of higher education via formal recognition channels, such as accrediting associations, local governments, and even the federal government. Corporations are now offering courses for collegiate credit; indeed, some have even founded colleges. Clearly, a dialogue must begin between the corporations and academe.

Reading this report will help both educators in the traditional sector and in the corporate sector achieve a common ground of understanding. Whereas industry's incentive is to guarantee that its employees know certain skills, institutions have missions defined over a more long-term basis. Each can learn something from the other, and the greater the degree of understanding, the less likely will counterproductive arguments occur.

Jonathan D. Fife
Series Editor
Professor and Director
ERIC Clearinghouse on Higher Education
The George Washington University

INTRODUCTION

Once distinct and separate educational delivery systems—
traditional postsecondary education and education provided by
employers (or "corporate education")—have begun to tread
some common paths. The essential point of merger is the formal recognition of postsecondary education institutions, programs, participants, and courses.

The purpose of this monograph is to clarify the relationship
between corporations and universities by focusing on what is
actually occurring in corporate classrooms and charting some
directions for mutual understanding between potential colleagues. Its thrust is to put corporate education into the context
of higher education. "Industry is. . .no less a segment of the
nation's educational system than our colleges and universities,
technical institutes, and other schools" (Lusterman 1977, p. 3).

Much of the literature on education and training in noncollegiate, primarily corporate, settings begins with the distinction
between education and training (Branscomb and Gilmore
1975), because for many years educators have viewed
corporate-sponsored instruction as training in the most limited
sense. This view no longer adequately reflects what goes on in
corporate classrooms, however. Precisely because of the expansion of corporate instruction into more traditionally delivered
education, in fact, college and university administrators need
to recognize instruction by employers.

The distinction between education and training should not be
construed too strictly, as the line between the theoretical basis
of knowledge and the practical application of knowledge is
very difficult to draw and the differences between training and
education have become less distinct. Four-year colleges that
started offering engineering and other applied programs were
thought to be too vocational and not worthy of an academic institution (Brubacher and Rudy 1976). The emergence of community colleges saw the award of associate degrees for many
types of vocational/occupational training. And in more recent
years, business and industry have started to offer courses for
college credit that had been considered to be solely the domain
of traditional higher education (Eurich 1985; Hawthorne,
Libby, and Nash 1983; Lynton 1984). If it were ever clear that
training belonged in industry and education in colleges and universities, it is not so today. Nevertheless, the terminology is
used interchangeably, because the delineation in actual practice
is not always clear.

The following terms are used throughout this monograph with the following meanings:

- "Corporate college" describes a degree-granting institution established by an entity whose major mission is something other than education.
- "Corporate education" means education offered by a business or industry for its own employees.

What is new in corporate education is that corporations, rather than relying on colleges and universities to offer credit-bearing classes and to grant degrees in areas of interest to business and industry, have increasingly begun to do so themselves. Rather than being a radical departure from previous practice, however, these efforts should be viewed as a logical extension of long-standing corporate activities. Unfortunately, the exact dimensions of corporate education are not known, but the history and current status of corporate education indicate a long-standing, extensive enterprise that includes considerable differences in delivery systems, depending on such factors as the nature of the industry, the size of the company, the extent of internal proprietary information, geographic location, and executive-level support.

The most substantive fact obscuring the distinction between educational services offered by colleges and universities and those offered by business and industry is the presence on the scene of American postsecondary education of a few institutions whose roots as educational organizations are somewhat unorthodox. These "corporate colleges" begun by noneducational entities offer collegiate degrees (Hawthorne, Libby, and Nash 1983). Of 3,000 institutions of higher learning identified in the United States (Carnegie Council 1980), 21 are considered "corporate colleges." While that number appears to represent a minor component, it is misleading, because behind the more visible corporate colleges looms the "shadow educational system" (John T. Dunlop quoted in Weeks 1975). Such degree-granting institutions (and the degree-granting proprietary institutions) are only the most striking feature of what has become the large enterprise referred to as "corporate education."

Several recent studies allow us to present the outline of this shadow educational system in terms of dollars spent, courses offered, and numbers and kinds of students served. These figures demonstrate that a diverse and widespread alternate educational system is indeed available to many working adults.

At present, formal recognition is conferred upon institutions by what has come to be known as the "triad"—the federal government, the state governments, and the private accrediting agencies. This report discusses recognition processes in postsecondary education, giving special emphasis to corporate education. It includes an analysis of issues surrounding recognition that are relevant to both traditional institutions of postsecondary education and the corporate educators.

The increasing interest in formal recognition by corporations suggests that an excellent opportunity exists to promote discussion between the two sectors to address a shared problem: how best to prepare Americans for work, to continue the education of workers, and to educate citizens who will live in a period of demographic, technological, and economic changes that are creating problems, stresses, and opportunities unparalleled in American history.

Corporate education is an extensive, multifaceted endeavor, costing billions of dollars, educating millions of people, and absorbing many working hours annually (Carnevale 1986; Carnevale and Goldstein 1983; Eurich 1985; Honan 1982; Lusterman 1977, 1985; Lynton 1984; McGehee and Thayer 1961; Miner 1977; Morse 1984). While few statistics are available to document this statement, several studies of corporate education, even though not precisely comparable, provide a general understanding of the practices in corporate education.

Cost

Estimates on the amount of money spent on corporate education vary greatly, and variations in cost accounting and record keeping are major reasons for the inconsistent data on cost (see Anderson and Kasl 1982 for a structure to standardize accounting procedures). Some companies, for example, consider the salaries and wages of trainees as a cost; others do not.

Diffuse accountability for training costs makes comprehensive cost accounting within a firm very difficult. Some expenses properly chargeable to education, such as travel to an outside seminar, can be buried in a travel budget. Some companies consider training strictly a plant or divisional function; thus, no companywide figures are available. In other cases, a central training unit charges other units per participant, but a systematic method to determine how much will be charged is not necessarily available. And the treatment of cost information differs when training is treated as an investment (Becker 1975; Flamholtz 1974; Schultz 1971) from when it is treated as a cost (the case in more traditional accounting procedures).

The magnitude of corporate spending on education—ranging from $2 billion annually (Lusterman 1977) to $20–40 billion annually (Lynton n.d.) to $100 billion (Gilbert 1976) to more recent estimates of $30 billion annually (Craig and Evers 1981; Morse 1984)—becomes clearer when it is compared to spending for traditional higher education. Combined federal, state, and local expenditures for public higher education in 1980–81, for example, were $31.4 billion (National Center for Education Statistics 1984). In 1985, all expenditures for postsecondary education in the United States were $94 billion, compared to $30 billion for formal employee education and $180 billion for informal, on-the-job employee training (Carnevale 1986).

Perhaps a more telling comparison is between two individual institutions. Before its breakup, AT&T's annual education and

Corporate education is an extensive, multifaceted endeavor, costing billions of dollars, educating millions of people, and absorbing many working hours annually.

training budget of $700 million was three times MIT's annual budget of $222 million. Of course, much of the education and training at AT&T is not comparable to the education at MIT; nevertheless, it is clear that institutions whose primary purpose is something other than education are spending amounts on education at least comparable to and often exceeding those spent at colleges and universities (Hodgkinson 1981).

Not all companies spend equal amounts on education and training, and not all industries invest similarly in employee education; furthermore, corporate training funds are spent on a variety of activities. The larger the corporation, the more it spends per employee on education and training. Because of their size, the largest corporations not only spend more per employee but also spend more in absolute terms. Further, larger corporations are more likely to spend money on in-house training and less on tuition reimbursement. The corporations that spend the most money clearly prefer to develop their own education programs.

Participation
Education across firms and industries is not comparable, nor do employees partake equally of education and training. The variance depends upon several factors: company size and type, the employee's job function, the type of course, and factors at individual companies. The industries showing the greatest rate of participation by employees are manufacturing, trade, transportation and public utilities, and construction (Carnevale and Goldstein 1983).

In 1975, approximately 13 percent of employees working in companies employing over 500 employees (4.4 million persons) took part in a company-sponsored course (3.7 million, or 11 percent, during working hours and 700,000, or 2 percent, after hours), and another 4 percent (1.3 million persons) took part in tuition aid programs. The percentage (13) is roughly the same for all companies with 1,000 or more employees but 10 percent for companies with 500 to 999 employees (Lusterman 1977).

In 1978, 6.8 million to 8 million employees participated in corporate-sponsored education and training (Goldstein 1982). And by 1985, participation among upper-level employees had increased (senior or upper-middle managers, 49 percent; middle managers, 66 percent; first-line supervisors, 72 percent; professional and technical employees, 63 percent) (Lusterman 1985,

p. 7), particularly in financial institutions. Those marked increases can in part be attributed to the deregulation of the banking industry, requiring employees to be more knowledgeable about new policies and practices.

Participation within firms varies, but generally participating employees represent a small portion of all employees within a firm—from 7 percent (Lynton 1984, p. 41) to 12.5 percent (Carnevale 1986, p. 20). Even so, those percentages mean that, by the beginning of the 1980s, an estimated 172 million employees attended a course provided by their employers (Adams et al. 1983).[1]

For white-collar employees, the participation rates are particularly high. A 1968 study estimated that 9 million out of 35 million white-collar employees (25 percent) would be exposed to some type of employer-provided training (Quackenboss 1969). In another study, 47 percent of all first-line supervisors and 46 percent of all middle managers participated in company-sponsored in-house programs (Miner 1977). Some companies require participation of all employees. In other companies, individuals are chosen on the basis of need or on supervisors' recommendations, usually for individuals being considered for promotion.

A substantial percentage of employees also attend outside courses. While the percentage is smaller for first-line supervisors, 10 percent or fewer attended professional or trade association meetings or job-related seminars, and 9 percent attended university-related programs lasting two to eight weeks. Middle managers were more likely than first-line supervisors to receive outside training: "Twenty percent or more attended professional or trade association meetings, 10 percent or less attended job-related seminars, and 26 percent attended university development programs" (Miner 1977).

Participants in corporate education are most likely to be 25 to 44 years old, with participation declining as employees age (Carnevale and Goldstein 1983, p. 56). The more education an employee has, the more he or she is likely to attend in-house training programs (p. 57). Technical and managerial employees account for 50.4 percent of trainees, even though they account for only 27.8 percent of all employees. Men receive more

---

1. As data are not available on the average number of courses employees attend in a year, it is impossible to generate a true figure of how many different employees take advantage of employer-sponsored education.

training than women, "consistent with the preponderance of men in most of the occupations likely to receive training" (p. 53).

Nonmanagement employees also receive training, although not to the extent that management-level (or those aspiring to management) employees do. In 8 percent of the companies in one study (Miner 1977), 100 percent of the employees participated in in-house programs during working hours. For another 8 percent of the companies, 50 to 80 percent of the employees participated in such programs. Ten percent or more of employees participated in in-house programs during company time in 41 percent of the companies. In an additional 16 percent of the companies, 10 percent or more of the employees participated in courses outside the working day (Lusterman 1977).

Top-level executives are far more likely than other employees to attend college and university courses. This participation is more likely in larger companies than in smaller ones, and in nonmanufacturing or nonbusiness companies than in manufacturing companies (Miner 1977). While managerial, professional, technical, and sales personnel in one study were educated predominantly by schools (66 percent), only 15 percent of such education was provided by formal company programs (Carnevale 1986). Overall, informal on-the-job training was the primary source of education and training for all other occupational groups (including service occupations, farming, forestry, and fishing, craftsmen, machine operators, and laborers). Retraining, however, was a more frequent application of formal company programs for all occupational groups.

Providers

Education for employees is provided in a number of ways: directly by firms for their own employees, by outside consultants, at college- and university-based seminars and short courses for management-level executives. Corporations generally pay for their employees to participate in such courses, but they also reimburse employees for courses taken at colleges and universities.

Corporations themselves, providing direct instruction to their employees, are by far the single largest provider of corporate education. In 1975, 80 percent of the money spent for education and training was spent on in-house company programs (Lusterman 1977). Eleven percent of that money was spent for tuition aid, 9 percent for other outside courses. The trend is toward widening the gap with more internal training (Luster-man 1985).

Various industries spend their education dollars quite differ-ently. Financial and insurance institutions spend 70 percent of dollars for education on in-house courses, 19 percent on tuition aid, and 11 percent on other outside courses. The industry that spends the second largest amount on employees' education—transportation, communications, and utilities—spends 87 per-cent of its money on in-house courses, 6 percent on tuition aid, and 7 percent on other outside courses. Wholesale and retail manufacturers, who spend the least amount on employees' edu-cation, spend 77 percent on in-house courses, 9 percent on tuition aid, and 14 percent on other outside courses (Luster-man 1977).

As might be expected, larger companies spend more money on in-house programs than smaller companies, for they have the resources and need to develop extensive in-house training and can do it most economically because of their size. Compa-nies with 10,000 or more employees spend 87 percent of their money on in-house courses, 7 percent on tuition aid, and 6 per-cent on other outside courses. At the other end of the scale, companies with 1,000 to 2,499 employees spend 43 percent of their education dollars on in-house courses, 33 percent on tui-tion aid, and 24 percent on other outside courses (Lusterman 1977). Because outside courses are expensive, some companies spend more on them than on in-house courses, although many fewer employees are involved.

While more companies have tuition aid programs available than other programs (Miner 1977), the reasons for the popular-ity of such a benefit have not been fully researched. Despite the number of tuition aid programs available, however, the rate of use of tuition aid is low, and the number of people attending in-house courses (generally offered during working hours) is much greater than those attending colleges or universities at their employer's expense (either during or after working hours) (Miner 1977).

Some of the education provided by firms for their employees is credit bearing; some is not. Courses taken under a tuition reimbursement plan are generally collegiate credit-bearing courses. Courses taken outside the firm—continuing education–type courses—may or may not offer credit. They are generally administered within workers' units rather than through person-nel or other centralized offices, although the practice varies.

The preparation of corporate trainers has changed in recent years, although not consistently so. Size of corporate training staffs has been increasing, with marked growth in financial institutions and less dramatic change in industrial firms (Lusterman 1985). Respondents in one survey indicate a growing interest in ''professionalizing'' the training function and reducing the number of individuals who rotate in and out of training departments. Firms pay more attention to specialization, usually in technical areas, while seeking specialists in program design, instructional design, and writing.

The growing use of sophisticated instructional technology stimulates the demand for individuals with special expertise (Office of Technology Assessment 1982). The demand in this area has in part sparked the beginning of degree programs in several colleges and universities at the baccalaureate, master's, and doctoral levels (American Society for Training and Development 1981; Hawthorne 1983).

The benefits and costs of using line managers (trained as educators or not) to provide instruction in specified areas continue to be discussed (Lusterman 1985), even as more line managers are being used in the delivery of educational services to corporate employees (Olson 1986).

Curricula

The curricula of corporate education run the gamut from basic remedial education (Lusterman 1977) to master's and doctoral degrees (Baker 1983; Eurich 1985; Hawthorne, Libby, and Nash 1983; Morse 1984), and courses vary in length from one-time sessions to extensive programs. Some training programs last three to four weeks (Lusterman 1977), while apprenticeship programs generally last two to four years. Other courses are roughly equivalent in length to a college semester.

In-house courses can be divided into three basic types: managerial, functional-technical, and basic remedial. Management development includes such courses as principles of management, management by objectives, and decision making. Functional-technical courses include production, sales, and computer literacy. Basic remedial education is just that: reading, writing, and arithmetic (Lusterman 1977).

More than half the companies in one survey offered courses in management development and the functional-technical area, while 10 percent offered courses in basic remedial education (Lusterman 1977). Twenty-seven percent of the management development courses and 21 percent of the technical-functional courses were 30 hours or longer, indicating substantial course content. Most of the money was devoted to and most of the students enrolled in functional-technical courses. Seventy-four percent of the total dollars were spent on functional-technical courses, and 61 percent of attending students took those courses. On the other hand, 24 percent of the dollars and 37 percent of the students were found in managerial courses. The remaining 2 percent of both money and students were in the basic remedial and other courses (Lusterman 1977).

Another survey found that the most frequently provided courses included supervisory skills, orientation of new employees, management skills and development, communication skills, and updating knowledge in technical skills (Zemke 1983). Yet another found that subject areas taught in-house are most likely to include business (59.1 percent of the firms in the survey), engineering and related fields (64.3 percent), personal services (59.7 percent), agriculture resources (65 percent), and interdisciplinary studies like basic adult education (87.7 percent) (Carnevale and Goldstein 1983).

Outside and after-hours courses tend to include broader subject matter than in-house courses offered during working hours. Of the companies surveyed by Lusterman, 39 percent offered after-hours courses. Most companies (36 percent of the total population or 92 percent of those offering after-hours courses) offered job- or career-related courses. Several more (5 percent of all corporations) sponsored basic and remedial courses, and 4 percent of all corporations offered courses on other subjects, for example, dressmaking, personal finances and budgeting, home and car repair (Lusterman 1977, p. 40). (Numbers total more than 39 percent because some companies offered more than one kind of course.)

Management and supervisory training courses include such courses as communications, human relations, decision making, planning, and problem solving. Data processing courses also vary, consisting of technical, programming courses for personnel who use the systems daily as well as courses in electronic data processing management for all levels of operational personnel. Many companies offer in-house courses in computer concepts for executives not directly involved in data processing (Quackenboss 1969).

Courses for managers and nonmanagers vary greatly. Courses for managers tend to be in areas such as employee relations, communications, wage and salary administration, and equal employment opportunity/affirmative action (Miner 1977), while courses for nonmanagers include an almost limitless number of subjects—from telephone courtesy and job skills specific to one industry to accounting, engineering, instrumentation, and mechanics (Miner 1978). Most courses are related to the job; very few companies offer courses in history and philosophy, although some do and also make available personal development courses in after-hours programs (for example, NCR's Owl College).

In some cases, managers take nonmanagement courses and nonmanagers take courses aimed at managers. A manager, for example, might take a course in computers, while many enrollees in management courses are being considered for promotion. The relationship between coursework and career progression is not clear, however, and merits additional study (Carnevale 1986).

Methods of Instruction

Although much corporate education is conducted using the traditional methods of lectures and discussions, the emphasis has been shifting "from presentation to show-and-tell to learning by doing" (Lusterman 1977, p. 54). This shift is a logical extension of the corporate complaint that college graduates are too oriented toward theory and deficient on practice; corporations are practicing what they preach.

Almost all of the companies offering in-house courses for managers use lectures and discussion (Lusterman 1977; Miner 1977). Ninety percent of the companies use films and videotapes; case studies, usually generated in-house, are another popular method (Miner 1977). Courses for nonmanagers tend to use more hands-on methods, following the early tradition of apprenticeship programs.

Corporations have established vestibule schools, separate areas in the factory set up like the factory. Workers can learn the skills they need without interfering with the work on the shop floor. Their advantage over a strict lecture arrangement is that students can immediately apply what they have learned, not only making the lesson more meaningful to the student but also providing instant feedback to the instructor on how well students have understood the lesson (Lusterman 1985).

Many companies use role playing to teach a wide variety of interpersonal skills, particularly to bank tellers, salesmen, and clerical personnel who interact with the public. Managers are taught how to interact with minorities and women in an effort to avoid discrimination suits.

Programmed instruction, done at the student's convenience, is another popular method (Miner 1977). It not only allows students to proceed at their own pace but also frees up time for the instructor to deal with problems. Because of the expense of video equipment, programmed instruction often uses primarily books, audio equipment, and computers, but the use of video equipment for firms with geographically scattered employees has been proved efficacious as well as economical (Kearsley 1977; Wells 1977).

A few firms (Texas Instruments, for example) use sophisticated instructional technology, such as satellites, to provide instruction to worldwide employees. Classrooms in many firms (for example, NCR Management College, Xerox, Bell Labs, Dana University) are equipped with state-of-the-art instructional technology, translation systems for foreign languages, audiovisual equipment, and computer equipment—both to learn from and about (see also Lusterman 1985; Morse 1984).

In addition, one-quarter of the companies in one survey had separate facilities dedicated to training, and another third had separate space (Peterfreund 1976). Some of the facilities, such as Xerox's training center in Leesburg, Virginia, resemble college campuses. In these and many other cases, attention to the ambience of the learning environment has been rigorous.

Organization

As might be expected, companies that spend a lot of money on training have established extensive, sophisticated organizational structures to administer their programs. Nevertheless, patterns vary from company to company. Some companies have training managers only at the corporate level, some only at the divisional level, some at both levels (Lusterman 1977). One study of 62 companies found that only three of them did not have anyone assigned to corporate education (Peterfreund 1976). Another study found that two out of five firms have employees who devote most of their time to training. The number of full-time, or almost full-time, trainers is large and has been estimated at 45,000 (Lusterman 1977).

Some large firms have separate education divisions, while small firms might employ only a single trainer. In most firms, education and training are part of the human resource development/personnel units. And more firms are including training in line managers' responsibilities (Lusterman 1985).

Evaluation

A range of attention has been paid to the evaluation of in-house courses. Some corporations spend little effort evaluating their educational programs, including cost effectiveness. ''In-house training appears to be exempt from normal managerial decision making, which is heavily cost oriented'' (McQuigg 1980, p. 324). Efforts to apply cost-benefit and similar economic analyses to managerial training in particular have had discouraging results (Jones 1971; Woodward 1975), in part attributable to the difficulty of costing benefits that are not readily translated into a scale with the financial investments in the program. Even though one economic evaluation (Kearsley 1982) and an in-depth study of evaluation methodology applied in a corporate management education program (Hawthorne *forthcoming*) merit attention, the focus for many corporations is need, not cost. If a corporation cannot find employees who can operate expensive, sophisticated equipment, it must train them to do so—regardless of cost. The alternative is lost capacity at the best and ruined equipment and industrial accidents at the worst.

Some firms, however, are actively involved in evaluation (Deere & Company, for example) (Hickerson and Litchfield 1978). Much of it is informal, but the more formal efforts include questionnaires, pre- and posttraining measurements of performance and/or knowledge, interviews, and supervisors' evaluations of the effectiveness of the courses immediately after the course and three to six months later (Miner 1977).

Early evaluation began with an interest in participants' comfort and satisfaction (''Was the room well-lighted?'' ''Were the chairs comfortable?'') at a period when much of the training was promoted as a privilege available to employees whom the company especially valued and in whom the company expected its investment to pay off. Much evaluation in the sixties and early seventies was conducted by psychologists, and the focus was on attitude and short-term acquisition of knowledge (Blumenfeld 1966; Blumenfeld and Crane 1973; Campbell et al. 1970; Clement 1981).

More recently, evaluating outcomes has been more seriously attempted (Hamblin 1974; Hogarth 1979), and different evaluation models are being applied to corporate education (Hamblin 1974; Kirkpatrick 1967, 1979; Stufflebeam 1974). The transition from primarily manual and production training to sophisticated instruction with a focus on management education has required more sophisticated methods of evaluation.

The current widespread interest in the evaluation of the impact of employee education on organizational productivity (Hamblin 1974; National Technical Information Service 1983, 1984; Office of Personnel Management 1979; Rittenhouse, Breitler, and Phillips 1980) increasingly involves supervisors of training program participants in the evaluations (Hogarth 1979). Multiple criteria are used more often than in the past, and group performance is being used as a criterion for evaluation in more firms (Lusterman 1985).

Applying evaluation strategies in corporate settings entails practical difficulties. While these difficulties have not been systematically explored, a key factor required for successful evaluation is the sophistication of the training manager with regard to evaluation. The amount of influence a training manager is able and willing to bring to bear to ensure full participation of all employees is a significant variable in successful evaluation and in the way in which (or whether) the findings are used.

How findings are used in a firm affects participation in later evaluations. Ten uses are most common: (1) to provide feedback to decision makers, (2) to improve the training program, (3) to gain knowledge of employees' skill levels, (4) to provide feedback to participants, (5) to build status and prestige for the training unit, (6) to study employees' effectiveness, (7) to analyze costs, (8) to identify future leaders of the organization, (9) to gain information for performance analysis, and (10) to place employees in units where they will be most beneficial to the organization's goals (Brinkerhoff 1981).

Corporate Colleges
The ultimate extension of corporate education is a degree-granting college. Generally, corporations have not taken that step, leaving credit- and degree-granting authority to existing colleges and universities. In some instances, however, corporations have founded degree-granting institutions or "corporate colleges" (Hawthorne, Libby, and Nash 1983) (see table 1).

A corporate college is an institution offering postsecondary degrees that was initially established by a nondenominational*

*Irving E. Dayton (Montana Commission of Higher Education), personal communication.

TABLE 1
CORPORATE COLLEGES

Name	Location	Original Sponsor	Receipt of Degree-Granting Privilege	Nongovernmental Accrediting Agencies*	Degrees Awarded
Manufacturing					
Chrysler Institute of Engineering	MI	Chrysler Corp.	1931		Master's[a]
			1983		Associate
	IL	Chrysler Corp.	1984		Associate
	MO	Chrysler Corp.	1985		Associate
GMI Engineering and Management Institute	MI	General Motors	1945	North Central, NATTS, ABET	Bachelor's
Institute of Textile Technology	VA	North American textile corporations	1944	Appl. SACS	Master's, Ph.D.
Institute of Paper Chemistry	WI[b]	Paper manufacturers	1929	North Central	Master's, Ph.D.
Philadelphia College of Textiles and Sciences	PA	Theodore Search, textile manufacturers	1955	Middle States	Associate, Bachelor's, MBA

Institution	State	Sponsor	Year	Accreditation	Degrees
Northrop University	CA	Northrop Corp.	1958	Western, State Bar of Cal.	Associate, Bachelor's, Master's, J.D.
Policy					
Rand Graduate Institute of Policy Studies	CA	Rand Corp.	1970	Western	Ph.D.
Insurance and Banking					
College of Insurance	NY	Insurance Society of NY	1962	Middle States	Associate, Bachelor's
American Institute of Banking	MA IL	AIB — Boston AIB — Chicago	1979 1985	Cand. N.E.	Associate Associate
Allied Health					
Institute of Health Professions	MA	Mass. Gen. Hosp.	1977	Cand. N.E.	Master's
College of Health Sciences	VA	Comm. Hosp. of Roanoke Valley	1982	Cand. SACS Cand. NLN	Associate
Bishop Clarkson College of Nursing	NE	Bishop Clarkson Hospital	1982	North Central, Appl. NLN	Bachelor's
Architecture					
Boston Architectural Center	MA	Boston Architectural Club	1979	National Arch. Accr. Bd.	Bachelor's

Table 1 (continued)

Management					
Institute of Management Competency	NY	American Management Association	Applied 1981		Master's planned
	CA		Applied 1982		Master's planned
Industrial Management Institute	IL	Midwest Industrial Management Association	1984	Plans to apply North Central	Associate
Arthur D. Little Management Education Institute	MA	A.D. Little, Inc.	1973	N.E.	Master's
Technical					
Stat-A-Matrix Institute	NJ	Stat-A-Matrix		Applying to N.J.	Master's planned
Wang Institute of Graduate Studies[c]	MA	Dr. An Wang (Wang Labs)	1981	N.E.	Master's
Other					
University Associates Graduate School of Human Resource Development	CA	University Associates	1979		Master's

Independent Proprietary

CIBAR Systems Institute	CIBAR, Inc.	CO	1974	Master's[c,d]
McDonald's Hamburger University[e]	McDonald's	IL	1985	Associate
Wholly Owned Proprietary[f]				
DeVry Institute of Technology	Bell & Howell (purchased 1967)	11 sites		
National Education Center	Private institution	FL	1984[g]	Associate
Watterson	Metridata	KY		Bachelor's
Katherine Gibbs	McGraw-Hill	MA, CT, other sites		Associate

*ABET = Accreditation Board for Engineering and Technology
NATTS = National Association of Trade and Technical Schools
NLN = National League of Nursing
SACS = Southern Association of Colleges and Schools

[a] Has had authority to grant Master's degrees in automotive engineering since 1931. Since 1967 provides internship sites and supervision, but students take coursework at local universities, from which they receive degrees.
[b] Has had degree-granting authority, but the degree students receive is awarded by Lawrence University.
[c] Merged with Boston University in 1987.
[d] No longer offers degrees; providing coursework only.
[e] Name is temporary; operating as a proprietary institution until degree-granting authority granted.
[f] Not an exhaustive list.
[g] The National Education Corporation purchased Broward Junior College in 1984.

entity, for profit or nonprofit, whose primary mission was something other than granting collegiate degrees. The primary interest continues to be in employers' creating colleges to develop, maintain, or upgrade their own employees' skills, even when nonemployees are allowed to enroll. The degree-granting characteristic moves corporate education out of a purely private arena into the public one.

A finer discrimination of what appeared earlier to be a simple phenomenon is called for, however, and this monograph therefore subdivides corporate colleges into corporate colleges that were established as nonprofit educational endeavors, those that were established as for-profit educational enterprises, and those that were purchased as for-profit educational endeavors. Proprietary institutions currently being developed and expanded present a different challenge to academe than nonprofit colleges and are worthy of additional study (Lynton 1984). While it is perceived that the bulk of proprietary schools compete in the same arena as community colleges, further research is necessary to understand better the arenas where different types of institutions operate.

The largest group, owned and operated by the National Education Corporation (NEC) in Newport Beach, California, offers courses in fields as diverse as robotics and advanced electronics and medical office management. Its annual revenues from industrial training are estimated at $12 million—in addition to NEC's 43 proprietary vocational schools that account for $115 million (*Fortune* 14 October 1985, p. 74). While two-year degree programs are the dominant type of program offered, NEC has recently sought to offer baccalaureate degrees, entering the arena with Bell and Howell's DeVry, Inc., and ITT's electronic schools (*Forbes* 17 February 1984, p. 117). Thus, a long-standing training business is moving more and more in the direction of the traditional nonprofit education system, and the interest in formal recognition by the proprietary schools merits attention by scholars and practitioners of postsecondary education.

At present, 21 corporate colleges in 11 states have degree-granting authority (excluding the wholly owned proprietary institutions). Almost all began by offering programs in specifically defined fields of study. For example, the Institute of Textile Technology offers programs only in textile technology, the Boston Architectural Center offers only architectural courses, and the Arthur D. Little Management Education Institute offers only a program in management for developing countries.

Chrysler Institute of Engineering began offering master's degrees in automotive engineering in 1931. Since 1967, however, it discontinued offering the degree, in part because of the high costs of facilities, and now serves as the site for internships for students enrolled in degree-granting programs at several metropolitan Detroit universities. Chrysler recruits the students; those who successfully complete the program can expect a job with Chrysler upon graduation. Since 1983, Chrysler has been granting associate degrees in a program built upon a certificate program begun in 1971 primarily to participate in job-training programs (like CETA and the Job Training Partnership Act) sponsored by the federal government (Morse 1984). Chrysler Institute also has degree-granting authority in Illinois and has applied for it in Missouri. Some divisions of Chrysler Institute are proprietary; others are nonprofit.

CIBAR Systems Institute in every way fulfills the definition of a corporate college except that it is proprietary. It was spun off from the parent corporation, a software development firm, in response to customers' requests for information about the development of software. The Institute offers a master's degree in software development and a certificate program. Several colleges throughout the country contract with CIBAR to teach the software classes for their students, who travel to Colorado Springs. In those cases, students earn college credit from their own colleges for classes taught by CIBAR. Several corporations also send their employees to CIBAR for classes.

The pattern of development of corporate colleges has been to begin with a single focus—generally meeting a corporation's needs—and over time to expand their offerings. Northrop University, for example, was begun as a technical training school for aircraft mechanics during World War II. It now offers a complex array of undergraduate and graduate programs, including a law school, and operates as an independent institution of higher education. The current bulletin of the Wang Institute of Graduate Studies refers to its software engineering master's degree program as its ''first'' program. While it is the only program, it does suggest that more are likely to follow.

Corporations have formed corporate colleges through the professional and trade associations to which they belong—like, for example, the American Institute of Banking and the Midwest Industrial Management Association. Almost invariably, the corporate colleges were formed to meet a need not filled by higher education. Wang Institute was founded when Dr. An Wang could not convince any Boston area colleges to offer a satisfactory degree program in computer software engineering,[*2] and the Institute of Textile Technology was founded and supported by textile firms to provide themselves with skilled researchers and managers.

On the other hand, the National Technological University was conceived of and developed by a consortium of colleges and corporations, not by corporations alone. It employs sophisticated technology to deliver education to participants electronically, suggesting a particular application for employees in sites that are rural or distant from colleges and universities. Participants in NTU are for the most part corporate employees. In that sense, NTU functions as a corporate college might. But the direct and active involvement of colleges and universities suggests a creative way to meet educational needs of employees in the context of traditional education (Eurich 1985).

Corporate colleges tend toward graduate or first professional degrees. GMI specializes in engineering, the Institute of Health Professions in graduate programs in nursing and allied health professions, and Wang Institute in computer software engineering at the master's level. The Rand Graduate Institute of Policy Studies offers just a doctorate, the Institute of Textile Technology only a master's and a doctorate, and the Arthur D. Little Management Education Institute only a master's degree. Once corporate colleges obtain degree-granting authority, they tend to seek accreditation, often because it is good business.[3]

*Cynthia Johnston (Wang Institute corporate liaison) 1982, personal communication.
2. Wang Institute affiliated with Boston University in 1987.
3. A slightly different twist can be seen in the background of the American College in Bryn Mawr, Pennsylvania. The American College began in the 1930s as the American College of Life Underwriters. For many years, it issued the Certified Life Underwriters certificate for insurance company employees. In the mid-1970s, the American College earned degree-granting authority from the Commonwealth of Pennsylvania and now grants a Master of Financial Services. At first look, this institution is a "corporate college." Despite funding in the beginning from insurance companies, however, the American College was started by a professor at the University of Pennsylvania because the nature of the education was viewed as inappropriate for an institution of the standing of the University of Pennsylvania. For purposes of discussion here, however, one might note that the American College was begun for the same reasons that the corporate colleges were begun, but not by employers (Eurich 1985).

Summary

Corporate education is a far-reaching enterprise, employing and educating thousands of people and spending billions of dollars, and traditional higher education has much to learn about it. Corporations are committed to their educational efforts, and they are likely to increase those efforts: The need for employee training is growing as a result of demographic changes, a decline in productivity per worker, impending shortages of entry-level workers, a higher proportion of poor and minorities, and more workers seeking self-fulfillment rather than simply job advancement (Carnevale and Goldstein 1983; Hawthorne, Libby, and Nash 1983; Morse 1984).

HISTORICAL DEVELOPMENTS

Employer-Sponsored Instruction

Corporate and collegiate education arose for different reasons, to serve a variety of social and economic needs. As time has progressed, however, they have moved closer together. While each has its special mission, the sharp distinction no longer exists that once existed between corporate training and collegiate education.

The earliest form of formal corporate education was the apprenticeship. Young men were apprenticed to a master craftsman, who assisted them to learn the skills required for the work the apprentice aspired to do. Transformation from an apprentice to a master was informal; no bar exams or CPA exams had to be passed (Rudolph 1962).

Factory schools and vestibule schools form the basis of corporate- or employer-sponsored instruction today. The focus of the earliest employee training was on technical skills for manual workers.

With the advent of the industrial revolution, the production of goods moved out of the home or the individual shop into the corporate factory. Preparing workers for a new kind of work necessitated a change in training methods. One response, in addition to on-the-job training, was factory schools. They were formed as early as 1872, the first by Hoe and Company in New York, which trained machinists to manufacture printing presses. Between 1872 and 1901, at least five such schools were established (Steinmetz 1976), and by 1916, over 60,000 young men were enrolled in such schools. When the National Association of Corporate Schools merged with the American Management Association in 1922, it was reported to have over 150 members (Clark and Sloan 1958). Soon such programs replaced apprenticeships as the mainstay of employee training.

The development of vestibule schools was influenced by the efficiency studies carried out by Gantt and by Taylor (Bendix 1956; Kelly 1919). Special job bosses in the plants generally conducted training sessions. (While women were frequently trained in these schools, they were trained only by women.) Productivity measures were used to determine the effectiveness of the training (Kelly 1919).

The first formal training program for salesmen was established by John H. Patterson, founder and president of the National Cash Register Company in Dayton, Ohio (now NCR, Inc.), in 1893 (Crowther 1923). Salesmen developed systematic sales methods in the field and communicated them to Dayton,

While each has its special mission, the sharp distinction no longer exists that once existed between corporate training and collegiate education.

where structured training materials were developed and classes conducted.

Attention turned from the training of blue-collar workers and salesmen to the training of foremen. A survey of companies offering courses in foremanship conducted in 1925 and 1926 reported that in 1924–25, 100 courses were offered but that one year later, 324 courses were provided to employees. By the 1920s, training of various types of employees by their firms was an integral part of corporate life.

An additional element in the story of corporate training is the formation of professional associations of individuals involved in training in industry. The National Association of Corporate Schools was begun by a group of 60 industrial educators representing 34 companies in 1913, who felt the need for such an organization because they did not get along with educators! In 1923, this group became the American Management Association (Steinmetz 1976). Other groups included the Petroleum Industry Training Directors (1939) and the American Society of Training Directors (1945), later to be called the American Society for Training and Development (ASTD) (Steinmetz 1976). The National Society of Sales Training Executives was started in 1940 (Craig and Evers 1981).

The depression brought with it a pronounced need to rehabilitate workers for new kinds of work (Davis 1933). The effect of the depression was not only its jolt of the economic and social order but also, in anticipation of future change, a recognition of the continuing need "to train employees so that they may be able to adjust when changes are necessary" (Davis 1935, p. 7).

The education of workers before World War II was, however, undertaken in quarters other than corporations and businesses. Strong involvement by labor unions has been a theme throughout the history of corporate education (Olson 1986, p. 34). In some cases, unions provided education directly, such as that provided by the International Ladies Garment Workers Union (Hader and Lindeman 1929). The federal government, with such peacetime programs as the Federal Emergency Relief Administration, the Smith-Hughes Act of 1917, and the Vocational Education Acts of 1946, promoted the education of workers. Colleges and universities—high schools, too—played significant roles in educating workers.

The beginning of World War II saw training opportunities for skilled and unskilled workers, retraining initiatives, and education in basic skills in place (Steinmetz 1976). World War II significantly affected the growth of corporate education, particularly as a result of the focus on education of management.

Two wartime programs in particular contributed to the development of education in industry—the Engineering, Science, and Management War Training (ESMWT) program, conducted by colleges and universities to train skilled professionals for wartime work, and Training within Industry (TWI). While the ESMWT program formed the basis of many contemporary collegiate continuing education programs (Steinmetz 1976), TWI was the genesis of management education in industry and had two major objectives: (1) to help plant managers train supervisors to improve their supervisory skills and (2) to increase the acceptance of TWI assistance by trainers and managers. One result of TWI that has had a lasting effect on corporate education in general and on management education specifically was the development of a cadre of professional trainers ("Training within Industry" n.d.).

Wartime dramatically affected corporate education (1) by focusing on the importance of training for work, (2) by mobilizing trainers from private industry in large-scale training where they developed training materials later used in peacetime, and (3) by exposing many workers at all levels to training in the context of work that needs to be done (Hawthorne *forthcoming*).

Following the war, the dominant type of employer-sponsored instruction was the orientation of employees—both employees new to the firm and current employees beginning new positions in the firm. Such training was developed to stem attrition as well as to foster loyalty to the company (Clark and Sloan 1958). While such training continues to be a common feature of corporate education, it hardly dominates the picture as it did after the war.

As World War II began, the United States had a voracious appetite for greatly expanded industrial output (Kane 1941). Early in the war years, leaders from government and industry recognized the need for highly skilled producers and for highly trained managers. With the new emphasis on the role of the manager, the emerging science of management as a field of inquiry supported by advances in theory in the behavioral sciences entered the scene (Likert 1961; Vroom 1964). The concomitant postwar growth in the size of corporations in a dynamic peacetime economy further nurtured the development of management education as available funds and differences in organization challenged old notions of management (Hawthorne *forthcoming*).

Many corporate executives had been trained in technical fields during the war and had had little coursework in the liberal arts and humanities. The focus of managerial education in the fifties, then, was on liberal education for top-level executives. It was thought that technically trained managers needed exposure to the liberal arts to develop into sophisticated corporate leaders (Clark and Sloan 1958).

Corporations themselves continued to provide more education for workers than training for managers (Clark and Sloan 1958). In 1946, the National Industrial Conference Board reported that "only slightly over 5 percent of 3,459 respondents reported having an executive training program" (Clark and Sloan 1958). General Electric established the first long-term internal executive education program, a nine-week program, in 1955 (Mahler 1976).

Management education became more widespread in the late sixties and early seventies, but not before colleges and universities had been the major source of such corporate education. Well-known programs offered by Harvard (the Advanced Management Program), Dartmouth, and Princeton led the way (Hawthorne, Libby, and Nash 1983).

The insurance industry was most active in educating employees in the postwar years (Training within Industry Foundation 1950). Training facilities within the industry doubled from the beginning of World War II to 1950 (Goodwin 1950, p. 15).

Corporate education is becoming more widespread and complex, and the literature notes the following dimensions in the structure of delivery systems:

- A movement away from programmed ad hoc courses to more individualized instruction (Peterfreund 1976);
- More full-time trainers (membership in the American Society of Training and Development was over 40,000 in 1985) (ASTD 1986a);
- Growing numbers of academic programs preparing corporate trainers (at, for example, the National College of Education, Northeastern Illinois University, and Johns Hopkins University) (ASTD 1981; Hawthorne 1983);

- A variety of expanded courses, including personal development, management education, sophisticated technical coursework, and remedial skills;
- More formal organizational arrangements for training (Peterfreund 1976);
- Assignment of permanent facilities for corporate training;
- Growing interest in evaluation (Hawthorne *forthcoming*; Morse 1984);
- Increasing use of collegiate terminology in corporate settings (Blount 1979);
- A growing attention to formal academic recognition, apparent in increased use of continuing education units (CEUs) by business and industry and growth of both the American Council on Education's and the New York Regents' programs on noncollegiate-sponsored instruction;
- The establishment of degree-granting institutions by noneducational entities like corporations and hospitals that offer associate, baccalaureate, master's, and doctoral degrees in such fields as engineering, architecture, and nursing (Eurich 1985; Hawthorne, Libby, and Nash 1983);
- Mounting use of instructional technology, such as Texas Instruments's satellite system and the use of computer-aided instruction at Hughes Aircraft (Morse 1984; Office of Technology Assessment 1982).

Collegiate Education in the United States: Preparation for Employment

The Puritan founders of Harvard College established the college in 1636 to ensure that the Massachusetts Bay Colony had educated gentlemen for the ministry and for public service (Brubacher and Rudy 1976). The Puritan ethic valued education because the ability to read the Bible was an act of godliness (Brubacher and Rudy 1976; Rudolph 1962). In such an environment, it is not surprising that a college was begun a scant 16 years after the first Pilgrims landed on these shores.

American collegiate education is rooted in the conviction that the country needs educated citizens for secular and religious service. While the classical curriculum of the colonial colleges (with one course of study that served all students) served for two centuries to educate community leaders (Brubacher and Rudy 1976), many economic, geographic, and demographic forces came into play after the Revolutionary War to cause a reexamination of collegiate education in the United States.

In 1817 in the Northwest Territory, Judge Augustus Woodward and some colleagues conceived of a university that was to serve as the capstone for the education system of the new territory. The university was to be financed from public funds to fulfill a basic tenet in Jeffersonian democratic thought: that a free society required an educated citizenry. It was not until 1837, a year after Michigan became a state, that Henry Phillip Tappan, the first president of the University of Michigan, embarked upon an innovation in education in the United States: a university that would serve any intellectually qualified student and would transmit knowledge of classical studies but would also prepare the student for a productive life as a citizen in a democratic society. Later, under James B. Angell, the University of Michigan would become one of the first universities in the country to offer a bachelor's degree in science and to institute programs in the professions (Peckham 1967). The programs at Michigan were considered to be equal in status to the classical curriculum characteristic of the private Eastern colleges.

Some colleges began to admit students to study scientific subjects, beginning with Princeton from 1796 to 1806 and Union College in 1802 (Rudolph 1962). The students at Princeton did not earn degrees but were given certificates of proficiency. To meet a perceived need for scientific military study and application, the United States government funded the U.S. Military Academy at West Point, New York, in 1802 as the country's first technological institute (Rudolph 1962). And in response to the needs of farmers to receive training and the benefits of research in the field of agriculture, the University of Pennsylvania organized a Faculty of Physical Science and Rural Economy in 1816 (Rudolph 1962).

The beginning of the nineteenth century ushered in other changes in collegiate education as well. The University of Virginia, the dream of its founder, Thomas Jefferson, was begun in part "to harmonize and promote the interests of agriculture, manufactures, and commerce and by well-informed views of political economy to give a free scope to the public industry" (Hofstadter and Smith 1961, p. 194). Ticknor at Harvard in 1825 urged that Harvard "follow the path of Continental universities, reform its system quite drastically, and strengthen its sciences and modern language" (Hofstadter and Hardy 1952, p. 23). Educated people were required to perform the work America needed. And if colleges failed to respond to the interests of business and industry, warned noted educational leader and Brown University President Francis Wayland in 1842, they would start their own colleges (Hofstadter and Hardy 1952, p. 24; see also Bronson 1914).

These positions are diametrically opposed to the landmark Yale Report of 1828 defending the classical curriculum and rejecting the inclusion of more mundane topics in a college curriculum. "The young merchant must be trained in the counting room, the mechanic in the workshop, the farmer in the field" (Rudolph 1962, p. 134). Following this lead, many colleges, particularly the Eastern schools, abandoned attempts to teach scientific subjects for a time.

The Morrill Acts of 1862 and 1890 provided for collegiate opportunities in the applied fields of agriculture and the mechanical arts (Brickman and Lehrer 1962; Johnson 1981; Veysey 1965). While it took until late in the century for the effects of the land-grant universities to be widespread, they marshaled in a period of dynamic cooperation between business and the university (Johnson 1981).

It was Andrew D. White at Cornell in 1868 who legitimized the worth of all types of education—science, humanities, or professional education. And the elevation of Charles William Eliot to the presidency of Harvard in 1869 (Hofstadter and Hardy 1952), the rise in graduate education, and the proliferation of professional schools within and without universities were all signs that American higher education was attempting to meet some of the needs of a busy country. The research initiated in colleges and universities modified colleges from institutions that merely transmitted knowledge (as the colonial colleges did) to ones that created it as well (Brubacher and Rudy 1976). Industry demanded it and the new wealth generated by American industry in the nineteenth century helped to finance it (Hofstadter and Hardy 1952, p. 31). The federal government participated in its first "research contract" with the Franklin Institute in Philadelphia in 1830 (Babbidge and Rosensweig 1962), setting the stage for funded research that has continued to ebb and flow from that time.

In the twentieth century, agriculture in addition to industry was to see that the new land-grant universities (and later other colleges and universities as well) were useful for training farmers but also for initiating advances in agricultural research (Johnson 1981). Thus began a relationship between colleges and businesses for promoting both pure and applied research and for educating and supporting both academicians and practitioners.

As the twentieth century progressed, "practical" education, such as accounting, gained equal status with the liberal arts and contributed to growing enrollments. While corporate interest turned toward employee education after World War II, the colleges and the universities were bulging with veterans earning degrees through the G.I. Bill. The 1960s spawned the community college movement and the further acceptance by colleges of studies that had previously been reserved for apprenticeship programs and the shop floor.

Throughout this period colleges and universities were growing so rapidly, particularly during the 1960s and early 1970s, that their attention to employee education was not extensive. They did, however, include executive education programs and the expansion of business colleges and their continuing education programs directed toward employees in the private sector (Morse 1984).

Summary
The nineteenth century saw the formation of patterns for collegiate education that reflect the adaptability, evolution, and diversity of American higher education (Ben-David 1972). In the current century, those patterns were again modified, remolded, and recast, but they moved from an inheritance of practicality and intellectualism, from transmitting knowledge to transmitting and creating knowledge, from the education of gentlemen to the education of citizens, from the preparation of public servants and ministers to the education of individuals so they can perform in a complex society.

Several factors contributed to the changing nature of American education: a growing interest in accessibility to higher education, the industrial revolution, the nineteenth century peaceful upheaval that changed the way of work and the workplace itself, and the technological revolution in the twentieth century that continues to challenge old standards about the work that is done and the way it is done.

The related histories of corporate and higher education demonstrate a recurring struggle to solve the problems of a dynamic democratic country while still holding true to educational ideals that have survived for hundreds of years. Woodrow Wilson, in his inaugural address as president of Princeton University in 1902 stated it well: American universities' task "is two-

fold—the production of a great body of informed and thought-
ful men and the production of a small body of trained scholars
and investigators'' (Weaver 1949, p. 65).

What is evident from this account of the efforts of corporations and universities is the independence of both as each struggled to address the same problems. At this time, the two
sectors of postsecondary education are converging—but not
necessarily cooperating—to address societal issues of education
for employment and citizenship throughout a lifetime. The next
section examines the points of convergence.

THE RELATIONSHIP OF CORPORATE COLLEGES TO TRADITIONAL HIGHER EDUCATION

Why Corporate Colleges Were Founded

The reasons that corporate colleges were founded mirror the growth of corporate education. Present corporate colleges were founded to meet a need not elsewhere addressed in postsecondary education. In some cases, the niche is one higher education might ultimately choose not to fill; in other cases, higher education belatedly realized the need and has taken steps to meet it.

Some corporate colleges were begun by companies to educate specialists for their industrial needs (Eurich 1985)—the Institute of Textile Technology, the Philadelphia College of Textiles and Science, and Northrop University, for example. The catalog of the Philadelphia College of Textiles and Science includes a brief history that illustrates the development of most corporate colleges.

> *Present corporate colleges were founded to meet a need not elsewhere addressed in postsecondary education.*

The Philadelphia College of Textiles and Science was founded in 1884 in the wake of the 1876 Centennial Exposition. A group of textile manufacturers, led by Theodore Search, noticed a sizable gap between the quality and variety of American textile products and those displayed by European mills. They set out to establish a school [that] would educate America's textile workers and managers. . . .

The school survived tough times during the depression, later entering a new period of growth at the onset of World War II. In 1941, the school was granted the right to award baccalaureate degrees and changed its name to the Philadelphia Textile Institute. . . . Facilities, programs, and faculty continued to grow in the '50s and '60s, reflected in yet another name change in 1961, to the Philadelphia College of Textiles and Science.

According to its bulletin, Northrop University was founded in 1942 as a "purely technical school," the Northrop Aeronautical Institute, to provide aeronautical technicians for the Northrop Corporation. It separated from the Northrop Corporation in 1953 and became an independent, private institution. In 1958, it received authority to offer the Bachelor of Science degree. It became the Northrop Institute of Technology in 1959 and was accredited by the Western College Association in 1960. Master's degree programs were added in 1969, and a school of law opened in 1972. The institute changed its name to Northrop University in 1975.

Just as the Institute of Textile Technology was founded by textile corporations, the Institute of Paper Chemistry was founded by paper manufacturers, and the College of Insurance was founded by the Insurance Society of New York. These three colleges have essentially stayed with their original missions. The Institute of Paper Chemistry has never awarded a degree, even though it is legally authorized to do so. Students earn degrees from St. Lawrence University.

As the histories of the Philadelphia College of Textiles and Science and Northrop University demonstrate, however, some corporate colleges expand from their original mission to offer nonspecialized programs. While their curricula tend toward the technical programs of their origin, they offer a diverse range of programs.

Other corporate colleges were founded to fill other needs. The Arthur D. Little Management Education Institute grew out of educational programs offered by Arthur D. Little for agricultural managers from developing countries. The institute specializes in (but is not limited to) instruction in management information needs, primarily for leaders from developing nations (Hawthorne, Libby, and Nash 1983).

The Wang Institute of Graduate Studies began when Dr. An Wang, founder of Wang Laboratories, could not get any colleges and universities in the Boston area to offer a master's degree in computer software engineering that was flexible enough to accommodate working engineers. Dr. Wang was convinced that a demand existed for skilled computer engineers, based on the needs of Wang Laboratories, and using the same entrepreneurial talents that built the laboratories, he started Wang Institute. Similarly, General Motors founded General Motors Institute in 1921 because a national shortage of engineers existed (Hawthorne, Libby, and Nash 1983).

Like Arthur D. Little Management Education Institute, other corporate colleges grew out of existing educational efforts of basically noneducational entities. The Institute of Health Professions, College of Health Sciences, and Bishop Clarkson College of Nursing were all founded by hospitals, which have long been in the business of training nurses but not of offering degrees. The American Institute of Banking arose out of internal education activities of the American Institute of Banking, one of the largest providers of noncredit corporate education (Hawthorne, Libby, and Nash 1983).

One corporate college was founded somewhat quixotically. The Boston Architectural Center grew out of an architects' social club and became a degree-granting institution in 1979. It has a volunteer faculty, a small paid administrative staff, and extremely low tuition (Hawthorne, Libby, and Nash 1983).

Some corporate colleges sprang up to address the same issues that have been offered as explanations for the growth of corporate education. The base of knowledge in the specializations taught by corporate colleges is expanding, in some cases through scholarship in the colleges and often in the original sponsoring corporation or corporations, which are likely to be on the cutting edge of technology. Furthermore, in many cases the equipment needed to educate workers is specialized and expensive. Traditional higher education is unable or unwilling to spend a large amount of money on equipment that will be used by only a few students; corporations have the equipment already.

Corporations looking to provide technical education, whether or not for credit, also have an advantage in terms of faculty. Many college professors need to be retrained, and some may not have ready access to state-of-the-art equipment or information when it is privileged information within a firm. In contrast, many employees of corporations are the individuals creating the new technologies. Further, colleges and universities in recent times face a shortage of faculty in the technical fields, partly because corporations pay better salaries (Main 1982) or offer better research facilities and no responsibilities for teaching. In the absence of alternative educational opportunities that corporations think they need, the corporations offer the coursework themselves.

Many corporate colleges are accredited. The North Central Association of Colleges and Schools has accredited the Institute of Paper Chemistry and Bishop Clarkson College of Nursing, the Middle States Association of Colleges and Schools the Philadelphia College of Textiles and Science and the College of Insurance. Some have received specialized accreditation: The Boston Architectural Center is accredited by the National Architectural Accrediting Board, Northrop University's School of Law by the State Bar of California.

How Corporate Colleges Differ from Traditional Institutions

Curricula

As noted earlier, corporate colleges—at least in their early stages of development—are more likely than traditional colleges to be specialized institutions (Eurich 1985). Most offer degree programs in limited areas, associated with the needs that led to their founding. Wang Institute offers only a master's degree in software engineering, although it also offers postdoctoral fellowships in Chinese studies. (According to its catalog, plans are underway to expand to other, related fields.) The Institute of Paper Chemistry and the Institute of Textile Technology specialize in paper chemistry and textile technology, respectively.

Some institutions have expanded their course offerings beyond their original mission (Eurich 1985; Hawthorne, Libby, and Nash 1983); Northrop University and the Philadelphia College of Textiles and Science, for example, offer a range of programs, although these institutions continue to offer degrees in fields related to their original missions. Northrop University, for example, which started by training aviation technicians, now has departments of aerospace, mechanical, and civil engineering; arts and sciences; business and management; computer and information science; electronic engineering; engineering technology; an institute of technology; and a school of law. Most of these departments follow the original mission; only the Department of Arts and Sciences and the School of Law cannot be considered outgrowths of the original technical program.

As a rule, corporate colleges have tended to stick to their original missions, and they are by and large not in competition with traditional higher education. They continue to offer programs that meet specialized needs.

Methods of instruction

Corporate colleges tend to emphasize practical skills as well as theoretical knowledge. Cooperative programs are common. General Motors provided cooperative placements and guaranteed jobs for GMI students from its founding until 1981. When General Motors withdrew direct sponsorship of the institute, over 300 companies or other organizations expressed an interest in sponsoring the institute and accepting its students in cooperative programs (Hawthorne, Libby, and Nash 1983). Other corporate colleges, like the Philadelphia College of Textiles and Sciences, emphasize cooperative programs.

According to its bulletin, Wang Institute requires specific skills before admitting a student to its MSE program, that is, at least one year of full-time work experience in software development. Prospective students for the Institute of Textile Technology must be referred by a textile manufacturer for admission.

Certainly many traditional institutions of higher education offer cooperative programs and hands-on experience; such programs are not limited to corporate colleges. And corporate colleges are interested in theory as well as practice; Wang Laboratories and the textile manufacturers did not have to found colleges to give their employees practical experiences. Corporate colleges expect their education to have more immediate benefit than many traditional colleges do, however, and this expectation influences their methods of instruction.

Flexibility

Many corporate colleges have schedules similar to those of traditional institutions. Some of them, however, do offer flexible scheduling. Wang Institute, for example, offers classes twice a week, in the afternoon, for one and one-half hours. Thus, adult workers have an opportunity to receive a master's degree. Not coincidentally, it also provides employers an opportunity to educate their employees without losing their services for an entire year. This factor was a primary reason why Wang Institute was founded; Dr. Wang was unable to convince a local university to offer part-time degree programs.*

Corporate colleges generally do not differ from traditional institutions of higher education in their faculty or requirements. The fact that so many of them have received accreditation testifies to their comparability to traditional colleges and universities. In addition, all of them have received degree-granting authority, some of them from states like Massachusetts that strictly monitor the granting of such authority. Where corporate colleges differ from traditional higher education is the narrowness of their missions.

Corporate colleges tend to hire more part-time faculty than traditional institutions of higher education. Not only do they re-

*Cynthia Johnston 1982, personal communication.

quire work experience as a requirement to teach, they also encourage their faculty to stay current in their fields by continuing to work (Eurich 1985). This approach is consistent with their emphasis on technological currency and hands-on experience.

The governance, structure, and academic and administrative titles of most corporate colleges parallel those in traditional colleges and universities (Eurich 1985). Their programs tend to emphasize specific academic disciplines, however. This approach reflects their understanding that real-world problems are usually solved by using the talents of individuals from a number of disciplines. It is also evidence of the willingness to be flexible shown by corporate colleges.

Corporate colleges frequently have no tenure policy. Instead, they operate on "a contractual basis with hours and salaries more comparable to the corporate business world" (Eurich 1985, p. 119). Whether this approach has implications for academic freedom remains to be seen.

The absence of departmentalism and tenure means that corporate colleges are better able to change curricula and requirements (Eurich 1985). Thus, corporate colleges find it easier to stay on the cutting edge of technology than do traditional colleges and universities, but it also subjects them to whims and vagaries, precisely what collegiate curriculum reviews were established to address.

Corporate colleges have been reported to be more likely than traditional colleges to regularly evaluate personnel and programs. This emphasis on evaluation is an outgrowth of established procedures of evaluation at most businesses (Eurich 1985), although it is an area that deserves considerably more research (Hawthorne *forthcoming*). These evaluations in many cases are designed to aid corporate colleges in seeing that they meet the need of their clients and students.

Why Corporate Colleges Will Continue
Momentum may suggest the beginning of additional corporate colleges. Of the 19 nonproprietary corporate colleges, six received degree-granting authority from 1970 through 1979; eight others received degree-granting authority since 1980. This recent phenomenon bears observation. It is possible that the number of corporate colleges may soon reach a point that will encourage the establishment of similar colleges.

The oldest corporate colleges still in existence were founded in 1929 and 1931. Presumably, these colleges have been meeting the needs of their constituents for over 50 years. As other corporate colleges arose from similar needs, it is not unreasonable to expect that their continued success might serve as models to other organizations with strong educational needs.

Some more concrete reasons exist for believing that corporate colleges will continue. Traditional higher education may legitimately decide that it cannot be all things to all people and choose not to offer some of the specialized programs offered by corporate colleges. The Institute of Textile Technology, for example, graduates very few students each year, but textile manufacturers are willing to make the large investment for the few students because they need their expertise and the fruits of the research conducted there. Traditional higher education might well decide that its money is better spent elsewhere, leaving highly specialized education to the corporations. Corporations will continue to invest in this type of education because they need it to be competitive.

Many corporations take pride in the education they offer, believing it superior to that offered by traditional colleges and universities. Even when corresponding education is available in the traditional sector, corporations choose to offer their own. It is often cheaper, more current, and more flexible (Hawthorne, Libby, and Nash 1983) and does not incur the costs of cooperative arrangements, which can be time consuming.

It is possible, of course, for corporations to offer education without directly competing with colleges by offering credit and founding degree-granting institutions. Indications are, however, that corporations will continue to formalize their educational programs (discussed in the next section). Briefly, however, corporations have found that offering credit motivates employees and provides them with an inexpensive fringe benefit (Hawthorne, Libby, and Nash 1983).

Corporations will continue to offer education and degrees because of the attitude of noncooperation, real or perceived, of traditional higher education (Luther 1984). Although colleges and universities have begun to cooperate with corporations, they have for the most part been reluctant to do so in the past. Several corporations that founded corporate colleges attempted to work with universities originally. Some even set up cooperative arrangements, which they found "less than satisfactory"

(Eurich 1985, p. 131). As long as this lack of cooperation persists, or is perceived to persist, corporations will continue to offer their own education.

Finally, a feeling is apparent, albeit undocumented, that higher education is losing some of its mystique. Conversations with corporate trainers reveal that corporations believe that it would be relatively easy for them to offer degrees if they choose to, but they choose not to because they do not consider themselves in the "education business." They are aware of corporate colleges and know that they are an option for them if they choose. Many underestimate the requirements imposed by states and accrediting agencies on degree-granting institutions and would find in practice that starting a college is not as straightforward as it might appear. Nevertheless, some corporations with successful education centers might decide that degree-granting authority is a logical next step for them, as it is clearly in no way the exclusive province of traditional colleges and universities.

PROCESSES AND PROCEDURES FOR RECOGNITION IN POSTSECONDARY EDUCATION

While the following discussion applies to traditional postsecondary education, it is also applicable to the corporate sector because corporate higher education's search for formal recognition indicates that once corporate entities request degree-granting authority, they tend to follow the same paths to seeking recognition that the traditional sector has followed. Before embarking on the description and analysis of the recognition processes and procedures and their implications for corporate education, however, a set of definitions is necessary.

Once corporate entities request degree-granting authority, they tend to follow the same paths to seeking recognition that the traditional sector has followed.

Definition of Terms

The legal recognition that is conferred by states is not necessarily an indication of quality of services or goods; it can merely mean a license to operate rather than an endorsement. Formal recognition has no common meaning in this country. No prediction is made of the relationship between the legal authority of an institution to grant degrees and the skills and knowledge the degree certifies. For most "reputable" colleges, of course, a degree does certify knowledge and experience. In states without special requirements for becoming an educational corporation, however, the degrees given by a few colleges certify only the paying of fees or a minimal level of instruction.

Legal recognition is conferred by a state in the form of a charter or papers of incorporation, giving the corporation authority to operate. Without this recognition, an entity cannot carry on its normal corporate business (hiring employees, raising money necessary to operate, for example). Requirements to obtain legal recognition as an educational organization vary from state to state.

Accreditation is not a legal form of recognition. It is the recognition conferred by a voluntary association by accepting into membership an institution or academic program that meets its standards. The most prestigious institutional accreditors are the six regional accrediting associations. Each recognizes institutions (in contrast to programs). Some specialized institutional accreditors also exist, such as the American Association of Bible Colleges. The accreditation process involves application by an institution with degree-granting authority, a self-review, and a site visit by a team representing the accrediting association. Standards of each of the six regional associations and the specialized associations vary, as does the consistency of application within and among the associations. The discussion here reflects the more common patterns (Harcleroad and Dickey 1975).

Specialized accreditation, also called programmatic accreditation and professional accreditation, is usually conducted by professional associations and trade associations (Glidden 1983). The American Dietetics Association accredits dietetics programs, for example. Professional accreditation may be done in cooperation with or separately from institutional accreditation by the regional associations (Kells and Parrish 1979). Occasionally, program accreditation is the same as institutional accreditation, as when the Association of American Law Schools accredits freestanding law schools (Young 1983).

Evaluation of courses is a recent phenomenon begun in 1974. Courses offered by noncollegiate institutions are evaluated for applicability as transfer credit that may be accepted by various traditional colleges and universities. Such courses are considered to be equivalent to a three-hour semester course. These evaluation programs are managed by the American Council on Education and the New York Regents, and both are nationwide in scope (Cross and McCartan 1984). Several state agencies cooperate with these programs in recognizing courses within their states (Pitre 1980).

State higher education agencies often evaluate public or independent institutions as a monitoring technique for the legislature and/or to aid the institutions (Bender 1983). This monitoring is important in states where the agencies prepare budgets or have the authority to approve or discontinue degree programs. State evaluations may not have the same binding effect that accreditation has come to have, except where the state has the authority to close the program.

Certification is conferred upon individuals by institutions and also by state agencies (for example, departments of education for teachers) and state boards.

Licensure is similar to certification but is legally binding and, where regulated, is required to do business. It is used primarily when a professional provides services directly to the public and is viewed as a protection for the public health and safety. Physicians, consulting engineers, and attorneys are licensed. Membership of licensing groups is comprised of professionals in the given fields as well as private citizens.

Patterns of Recognition

The legitimate recognition of higher education in this country is complicated because no central recognizing agency exists. Not only do both public and private recognizers exist; those public and private recognizers exist at the state, regional, and federal levels. Further, they recognize not only institutions but also programs, courses, and individuals.

Patterns of recognition can be formal or informal. While the two frequently accompany each other, they are not the same, partly because the different recognizers legitimize at several levels within the educational "system" with various forms of recognition for various purposes and uses at different times (Young 1983). Informal recognition may give an institution prestige; formal recognition gives an institution certain tangible benefits.

Finally, recognition can be voluntary. Some prestigious institutions do not seek specialized accreditation (for example, Juilliard is not accredited by the National Association of Schools of Music) but instead rely on the public perception of their quality to attract and maintain faculty, students, and institutional resources.

Formal recognition

Higher education in the United States has been recognized by what has come to be known as the triad (Kaplin 1975): the state governments, the federal government, and the voluntary accrediting associations.

The state governments bear the primary responsibility for chartering institutions of higher education. All institutions must be granted a corporate charter by their home state. Some states require only that the institutions comply with their law governing nonprofit corporations; others have more stringent requirements (Bender 1983). The diversity of state requirements is illustrated in table 2 (see also Appendix A).

To examine the actual ways in which corporate-sponsored education is extended legal recognition, the authors conducted a survey of state higher education boards (including Washington, D.C.) to determine what approach, if any, they had taken regarding noncollegiate institutions' requests to grant degrees. Thirty states responded to the survey. Five more states referred to other agencies, which were sent follow-up letters. Two of those five agencies responded. Therefore, 32 of the 50 states and the District of Columbia responded (a response rate of 63 percent).

The summary results on table 3 show that only one state, Massachusetts, explicitly regulates noncollegiate institutions. A telephone survey of some of the states that sent their regula-

TABLE 2

SUMMARY OF STATE STATUTES ON DEGREE-GRANTING AUTHORITY[a]

Final Authority Granted by Legislature	Degree-Granting Authority Delegated to Higher Education Board by Legislature[b]			Operation in State Permitted by Nonprofit Corporation Laws	Other
Connecticut[c]	Alabama[d]	Kentucky	Ohio	Arizona	Hawaii[f]
Maine[c]	Alaska[d]	Maryland	Oklahoma[d]	Iowa	
Nevada	Arkansas	Massachusetts	Oregon[d]	Louisiana	
New Hampshire[c]	California[d]	Michigan	Pennsylvania	Missouri	
	Colorado	Minnesota	Rhode Island	South Dakota	
	Delaware	Mississippi	South Carolina	Utah	
	District of Columbia	Montana[d]	Tennessee[d]	Wyoming	
	Florida[d]	Nebraska	Texas[d]		
	Georgia[d]	New Jersey	Vermont[d]		
	Idaho[d]	New Mexico[e]	Virginia		
	Illinois	New York[d]	Washington[d]		
	Indiana	North Carolina	West Virginia		
	Kansas[d]	North Dakota	Wisconsin[d]		

Note: Within each category, a great deal of variability exists among states.

[a]Some states do not explicitly regulate degree-granting authority but do regulate who is allowed to operate a postsecondary educational institution.
[b]A typical state statute delegates the regulating of degree-granting postsecondary institutions to the named agency.
[c]The higher education board of the state makes recommendations to the legislature.
[d]The state excludes accredited colleges from some or all of the postsecondary legislation.
[e]The state has the power to regulate institutions but does not have the power to give degree-granting authority.
[f]State law requires that institutions must indicate whether or not they are accredited.

TABLE 3

SUMMARY OF STATE REGULATIONS OF HIGHER EDUCATION BOARDS ON NONCOLLEGIATE DEGREE-GRANTING INSTITUTIONS*
(Winter 1984)

Explicitly Regulates Noncollegiate Institutions	Regulates Private Educational Institutions		No Regulation
Massachusetts[a]	Arizona	Minnesota	Alaska
	Arkansas[b]	New Hampshire[a]	Alabama
	California	New Jersey	Idaho
	Colorado[a]	New Mexico	Indiana
	Connecticut	New York[b]	Iowa
	Delaware[a]	Nevada	Louisiana
	Georgia[a]	North Carolina[a]	Mississippi
	Illinois	Pennsylvania[b]	Missouri
	Kansas	South Carolina	Montana
	Kentucky[a]	Texas[a]	Nebraska
	Maine	Virginia[a]	Oklahoma[c]
	Maryland	Washington	Oregon
	Michigan	West Virginia	Rhode Island
			Utah
			Wisconsin
			Wyoming

*The District of Columbia, Florida, Hawaii, North Dakota, Ohio, South Dakota, Tennessee, and Vermont did not respond.
[a]These states also use accreditation as a standard.
[b]These states would require corporations to comply with the law governing nonprofit corporations.
[c]This state recognizes only advanced standing credit from noncollegiate institutions.

tions for private institutions revealed that they would treat non-collegiate institutions in the same manner as they regard traditional privately supported institutions.

The federal government recognizes institutions for the purpose of dispensing federal monies, mostly student financial aid. It does so by stipulating that for a student to receive federal financial aid, that student must be enrolled in an institution accredited by an accrediting agency approved by the Department of Education (Chambers 1983), and that stipulation has contributed to the proliferation of private accrediting agencies (Bender 1983). Because accreditation is a voluntary activity and many fine institutions are not, by their own choices, accredited, the Department of Education has also had to seek equitable ways to acknowledge the nonaccredited institutions. Among such attempts is the "three-letter rule," under which a nonaccredited institution can be listed by the federal government if it submits letters from three other institutions indicating that they accept transfer credits from that nonaccredited institution. That rule was subsequently revised to recognition of institutions who were candidates for accreditation, whether or not they would ever be willing or able to become accredited (Chambers 1983, pp. 247–49).

Several types of accrediting agencies exist. The most prestigious are the regional accrediting agencies, such as the North Central Association of Colleges and Schools, that accredit institutions (but not institutions without state degree-granting authority). Other accrediting agencies include the National Association of Trade and Technical Schools, which accredits institutions, and the National League of Nursing, which accredits programs. "COPA [the Council on Postsecondary Accreditation] ha[s] recognized 51 accrediting bodies and ha[s] identified more than 70 additional organizations that were operating without recognition" (Young 1983, p. 9).

Institutional recognition. Each institution organizing for the first time must be incorporated and receive degree-granting authority from a state. Many states have established standards that institutions must meet before they can receive degree-granting authority: standards for educational resources, mission statements, faculty, and fiscal solvency, for example. No further legal requirements must be met for institutions to operate, but most of them seek regional or other institutional accreditation, which entitles them to become eligible for federal funds and makes it easier for their graduates to transfer and/or attend graduate school.

If an institution has been accredited in one state, it may be able to offer degrees in another state (see table 3 and Appendix A). It is not possible to skip the states entirely, however, because the regional associations do not evaluate an institution unless it has degree-granting authority (Bender 1983; Young and Chambers 1980).

Recognition of programs. In some states for some fields of study, institutions must receive state approval to offer certain programs. For some professions, state approval of a program commits the state to certify the graduates (Spurr 1970). In other cases, completion of the program only entitles the graduate to sit for a state-prepared examination. Program standards are set by a specialized licensing board or by a professional association that has been delegated that authority by a licensing board (Dickey and Miller 1972). Professional accrediting associations generally do not accredit programs unless the institutions offering the programs are regionally accredited (Orlans 1975).

Recognition of courses. Evaluation of courses is a relatively new phenomenon that started with ACE's evaluation of courses offered by the military during World War II. That program led to its current evaluation program. ACE (and/or the New York Regents) evaluates courses given by noncollegiate institutions like military bases, corporations, and hospitals. (The present programs were begun jointly by ACE and the New York Regents but soon after split into two programs.)

These two groups can only recommend credit; only colleges can award it. To the extent that the organizations offering Regents- and ACE-evaluated courses are not degree-granting institutions, they have bypassed state procedures entirely, which presumably is compensated for by the fact that the institutions accepting the courses and granting the degrees have been approved by the states. Some Regents-approved courses have been used for licensure (Regents 1983). ACE has also established a National Registry of Credit Recommendation, which includes only courses that ACE has evaluated and has recommended for credit. The registry provides students with a transcript showing courses passed, course content, and credit recommendations. It can be used by employees wishing to seek credit from colleges and universities for courses taken at their corporations (Eurich 1985).

These procedures illustrate that the recognizers rely to a great extent upon each other. So long as each recognizer performs adequately and stays within its jurisdiction, the system functions well.

Recognition of individuals. If an individual wishes to practice a licensed profession, he or she must usually first complete an accredited program. (Some states still permit people to sit for examinations without attending college; in Virginia, for example, one can still read for the bar.) The licensing authority or the specialized accrediting association approves the programs.

A strong relationship exists between requirements for licensure and professional accrediting (Parrish 1980). Once the individual has received the license, he or she may or may not be accepted in states other than the one that granted the certification. Occasionally, the education received entitles the individual to take the examination in that state only (Kirkwood 1978), but in some cases, individual states have arranged reciprocity agreements. Many state licensing boards whose members are predominantly professionals (practitioners and academics) in the given field generally require attendance at accredited institutions for certification or licensure.

Informal recognition

Informal recognition consists of recognition of reputation in the marketplace. Informally, students recognize institutions, programs, and courses through the demand for and support of the educational components. In fact, a large percentage of educational change can probably be linked to the supply and demand generated by students' recognition as institutions seek to meet society's needs.

Employers recognize educational institutions through their demand for students, as shifts occur in the labor force, the economy, the political environment, and technology. Foundations and other resource providers recognize educational institutions through their economic decisions regarding the allocation of scarce resources. Other institutions recognize them through the acceptance of credits obtained by mobile students. While such recognition can occur formally, through interstate and intrastate articulation agreements like Florida's course numbering system, the degree of informal recognition given by these groups can depend on the degree of formal recognition obtained by the entity.

The Current Status of the Recognition Of Corporate Education

Although the first corporate college to receive degree-granting authority was incorporated in 1929, the widespread formal recognition of corporate education is more recent. Much of this recognition is granted by colleges and universities themselves rather than independently through the mechanisms described earlier. Some corporations, for example, offer courses only to their own personnel, taught by their own personnel, for which credit is awarded by a neighboring college. In many cases, this type of arrangement has worked satisfactorily. The corporation ensures that its employees are educated to meet its needs, employees receive education and college credit, and the college receives money and the potential for more students seeking degrees using their credits.

This type of program has its limitations, however. Some colleges are reluctant to give credit if they do not know the quality of the instructor or if the instructor does not have a terminal degree. Some colleges are opposed in principle to limiting courses to employees at a single work site. Some corporate courses are not suitable for college credit or are not given in time frames or modules that fit well into the college's academic calendar.

Corporations have found other ways to see that their students receive credit for courses. As stated, both the New York Regents and ACE evaluate courses and recommend them for credit. While their recommendations are not binding on colleges, studies conducted by the Regents have shown that evaluated corporate courses have a high rate of acceptance. During academic year 1975–76, 469 students received credit for corporate courses, and 82 percent of the courses they requested credit for were approved. Seven percent of the students used corporate courses for licensure or certification (McGarraghy and Reilly 1981). The ACE National Registry can be used to facilitate this process.

The reactions of the states to corporate colleges varies. New York actively discourages corporations from founding colleges and encourages them instead to cooperate with traditional collegiate institutions.

Illinois requires the colleges to offer a specified percentage of general education and cognate courses but assists corporations seeking to establish degree-granting institutions. Massachusetts requires an independent board of directors. The authors' survey of state higher education agencies found that most states have not yet faced the question of corporate colleges.

Additionally, the increased tendency of colleges and universities to give credit by examination and to accept experiential learning for credit means that corporate educational experiences are more likely to be given college credit. College registrars and admissions officers have indicated a greater willingness to give credit for corporate education (Pitre 1980).

Why Corporations Seek Recognition

American society has become an increasingly credential-conscious society, and the "certifying effect" (De L'Ain 1981) has continued to grow in importance. Employees are reluctant to invest time and effort in education unless they will receive credit (Mayville 1972). Corporate executives have observed that enrollments and attention increase once a course has been evaluated and receives a recommendation for credit. Once employees take such a course, they are more likely to take other courses, both in-house and in colleges and universities (McQuigg 1980). Corporations see obtaining recognition for courses as a method of inspiring employees to do willingly what the corporation would make them do anyway.

Not all employees are reluctant to take courses; some wish to learn or to improve their skills and enhance their opportunities for advancement. Even employees who learn willingly, however, like receiving academic credit for their efforts. When employees find that the courses they have taken at their places of business will get them credit at a local college, they are often motivated to enroll at that college and earn a degree. Not only do they have a head start because of their credits; many now have the confidence that they can compete at the college level.

Once ACE or the New York Regents approve a course, corporations feel their courses are the equivalent of college courses. In fact, corporations are likely to perceive of their courses as better than college courses because they offer individualized instruction, modern equipment, and a practical as well as a theoretical component (Cross 1981). Corporations believe that they are now conducting a substantial amount of the education of today's work force. According to the National Center for Education Statistics, employers are educating at least 11 percent of adult workers (Carnevale 1986). Business firms provide 14 percent of all training in the United States, more than any other nonschool organization (p. 23).

Therefore, corporations believe, the federal government should shift a substantial amount of available training funds to them (Maeroff 1981). In fact, the Job Training Partnership Act (JTPA), which earmarked most training funds for businesses and limited the role of educational institutions, acknowledged the amount and quality of training done by business and industry (P.L. 97–300, 13 October 1982). The dominance of the private sector in the Private Industry Councils established by the JTPA also created "a vehicle for increased employer influence on all education and labor policy decisions'' (Olson 1986, p. 35).

Other proposed federal legislation that provides funds for training and retraining includes the Trade Adjustment Assistance Extension and Reform Act, which would supply training vouchers for workers who lose their jobs to competition from foreign trade. Funds have come from a tax on imported goods. If the National Training Incentives Act (H.R. 1219) is passed into law, corporations would obtain tax and other benefits to encourage educational initiatives (ASTD 1986b). Furthermore, ASTD, the largest professional association of trainers in industry, is supporting federal legislation to use the tax code to encourage more training by employers. Of relevance here is that ASTD will vigorously oppose ''any proposal compromising the employer's prerogative to create training in-house or to choose outside suppliers of services'' (ASTD 1986b).

In the past, many corporations did not seek recognition of their educational activities from the higher education community because, in fact, the idea never occurred to them. When it was clear that formal education could be obtained only in a college, often in a residential collegiate institution, the question of recognition for corporate education never arose, even though corporations were providing educational services to their employees at many levels. The advent of nontraditional education changed the focus. What became important was what one learned, not where one learned it (Keeton 1980). Students received credit for corporate education through external degrees or placement examinations before corporations began to apply for credit themselves (Goldstein 1980). When it appeared that some corporate education was equivalent to collegiate education—through its acceptance by some collegiate institutions— the next steps to recognition no longer seemed revolutionary. This fact does not imply that all corporations with educational programs are moving in this direction, however, although the increase in corporate courses gaining approval (Regents 1977), the advent of the corporate college (Eurich 1985; Hawthorne, Libby, and Nash 1983), and the growing role of corporations nationally in the training business suggest some movement in that direction.

Still colleges retain much of their luster, and even large companies with extensive training programs like Xerox and AT&T (Lusterman 1977) prefer to rely on colleges to do most of the education—so long as colleges meet their needs. Others, like

General Electric, have indicated that they have thought of offering their own degree but do not because the geographical spread of their many locations, no one of which has enough interested employees to justify a corporate college, makes it infeasible. Honeywell has begun to send its engineers through GE's master's level program, because management thinks it is of higher quality than comparable collegiate programs (Pitre 1980). If a sufficient number of other companies send their engineers to GE's master's program for their graduate coursework, it might well become desirable both economically and educationally for the corporation to begin offering degrees.

Corporations' decisions about whether to offer degrees themselves or to work with traditional higher education will depend in large part on the response of traditional higher education to their needs and the direction of tax dollars for a range of educational initiatives. And they will raise a number of issues regarding recognition for traditional higher education.

Issues Involving Accreditation

Corporate colleges bring into sharper focus some issues involving accreditation that have been the subject of debate in recent years: a focus on output, including learning outcomes, concern about the impact of the profit motive on institutions, and the need for the independence of governing boards.

Historically, accreditation has focused upon input—the things like quality of faculty and number of books in the library that go into making a college (Andrews 1979; Dickey and Miller 1972; Green 1981). The theory was that high-quality input necessarily led to high-quality education. This theory was challenged by two movements: nontraditional education and the measurement of outcomes. Nontraditional education generally included assessment for prior learning and unusual delivery systems—Empire State University, education at military bases, and contract learning, for example (Andrews 1979). Corporate education easily fits into a number of nontraditional categories. The courses were taught off-campus, often by instructors without doctorates. The length of a course varied depending upon the amount and type of information and the needs of the corporation, and frequently courses did not fit into an academic calendar. Some of the courses were taught by professional organizations, such as the American Management Association.

The growth in nontraditional education caused the Council on Postsecondary Accreditation to take a look at the accreditation of nontraditional education. That study resulted in several recommendations. One was that "institutional accreditation should operate in a single mode that will accommodate all of postsecondary education, recognizing both process and performance components in the evaluation of institutions" (Andrews 1979, p. 344).

This movement paralleled the movement toward the measurement of outcomes (Astin 1977; see also Bowen 1977 and Dressel 1976), which stated that what was important was what students learned and how they changed as a result of the college experience, not what went into the institutions. The movement also appealed to corporate educators, who have for a long time contended that the outcomes of their education, as measured by students' knowledge, was superior to that of traditional higher education, even if some of their inputs, such as faculty degrees, were lower. They were aided in their argument by research showing that traditional indices of institutional quality do not seem to contribute to students' overall development (Astin 1977).

Both these movements will play significant roles in higher education for the foreseeable future. Corporate education, as a sector of nontraditional education, will continue to grow. The incorporation of outcomes measurement as part of the accreditation process will enable corporate educators to demonstrate their worth while giving accreditors a basis for evaluating their efforts.

Most corporate colleges were established to provide trained and educated employees for a firm or group of firms. Thus far, too, corporate colleges have chosen to apply to the traditional and mainstream accreditors and are operating in only a few states. Because many states have no clear provision for dealing with this kind of educational initiative by noneducational entities, two related issues are relevant here.

The first is the issue of control. To what extent should the institution be independent of the corporate founder(s)? The second has to do with the curriculum allowed by recognizers. A collegiate governing board that was under the control of the corporate board would be more likely to make financial decisions for the sake of the corporation than for the institution. An independent board is also more likely to protect academic freedom in teaching and research than to try to dictate a curriculum based upon immediate corporate needs. Again, accrediting agencies are in the best position to guarantee this independence, although state governments, through the chartering process, can also do so.

Of concern is the possibility that institutions begun with narrowly defined goals that remain under the control of the corporate founders would confine their offerings to a limited selection of courses and workshops designed to meet short-term corporate goals instead of providing a broad-based education. Degrees from such institutions would not be comparable to traditional collegiate degrees. It was this fear that led the regional accrediting associations to deny accreditation to proprietary institutions, a stance upheld by the federal courts in *Marjorie Webster Junior College* v. *Middle States Association of Colleges and Secondary Schools* [302 F. Supp. 459 (1969); 432 F.2d 650 (1970)] (see also Kaplin 1975). Of course, this action only led the proprietaries to start their own accrediting association, which has received recognition from the U.S. Department of Education. The corporate colleges could presumably found their own accrediting association as well.

In fact, the appeal of formal recognition led to the formation of an accrediting association in 1974, the Council for Noncollegiate Continuing Education (CNCE), which is listed by the U.S. Secretary of Education. This association "provides accreditation and evaluation services to the noncollegiate, noncredit field" (CNCE 1985, p. iv). Educational corporations, labor unions, corporate in-house training departments, public affairs and cultural societies, and government agencies, among others, are eligible to apply for accreditation by CNCE.

The accreditors who have always been interested in the issue of adequate financial support might be well advised to accredit institutions that are adequately financially independent from their corporate founders, allowing them to provide programs comparable in every way to degree-granting institutions, no matter their origins.

Approaches to the Recognition of Corporate Education

Although programs and courses are subject to the processes of recognition, the major issues concerning recognition arise in an institutional context. When a corporation offers a single course or a series of courses, it generally does so only because it has an interest in training individuals in a specific area. Those courses carry no recognition outside the firm. It is true that sometimes colleges or universities choose to give credit for the courses, either by assisting in the choice of the instructor or by granting post hoc credit under an established program that evaluates courses. The choice of whether or not to grant credit, however, remains with traditional higher education.

This report deals with the issues of institutional recognition and program recognition as one. Programs are accredited only in an institutional setting, whether the programs are part of a larger institution or are freestanding. For purposes of simplicity, this discussion is limited to the recognition of corporate colleges.

Accreditation began with the question, What is a college? (Young 1983). Today the question is, What is an institution of postsecondary education? The issues concerning the recognition of corporate colleges can be examined in this latter context.

Institutional quality

The issues surrounding institutional quality focus on three areas: governance, finance, and curriculum. In this regard, corporate colleges are no different from traditional colleges where the same issues pertain; observers, however, place different emphases on these issues when corporate colleges are involved.

Governance. It has long been the tradition in the United States that academic institutions are governed by lay boards (Rudolph 1962). Accreditation standards generally provide that a separate governing board be provided, with some, though not necessarily a majority, public members, the purpose of which is to protect the institution from undue political or religious influence (Southern Association 1977).

An educational institution governed by a corporation is only one segment of an organization with many interests. If the governing board of an institution were identical to the governing board of a corporation, the potential would exist for sacrificing the educational institution to the larger interests of the corporation. This issue becomes more complex when the educational institution is expected to make a profit.

The two recognizing entities with the most experience in this area are the Massachusetts Board of Regents and the New England Association of Schools and Colleges. As noted in table 1, five of the corporate colleges are located in Massachusetts.

At the time Massachusetts General Hospital (MGH) applied for degree-granting authority, the Massachusetts Board of Higher Education (now the Regents) did not have a policy to respond to noncollegiate institutions (Stevens 1977). Because the Board of Higher Education was concerned with the problem of governance, the board of MGH passed a resolution guaranteeing academic freedom to the educational component at the hospital.

The issue of governance is related to the issue of finance. Some are concerned that a governing board tied too closely to the sponsoring institution will not protect the financial integrity of the institution.

Finance. The concerns about finance are twofold. The first is that the corporation may use the educational institution to make money. A countervailing argument, however, is that the profit motive might cause the institution to use its resources more efficiently, which would lead to higher-quality education (see *Marjorie Webster* v. *Middle States Association*).[4]

The second concern is that the corporation may withdraw financial support from the institution when support is no longer cost beneficial or when the corporation does not need the particular training any longer. Adequate finances have long been a concern of accrediting associations, and many otherwise worthy institutions have not been accredited because they lack adequate financial resources.

While the financial stability of institutions is important, two factors militate against being unduly concerned about corporations' wholesale abandonment of their educational institutions. Generally, a corporation will not make the enormous investment necessary to begin an institution if it does not intend to sustain it. Although General Motors has withdrawn direct sponsorship of General Motors Institute (after more than 30 years of support), GMI is now established enough that it has had no difficulty in securing substantial funding from other corporations (Eurich 1985; Shellum 1981). Further, as traditional public and private higher education now faces the possibility of closure, corporate colleges cannot be held to a higher standard than other institutions of higher education. The requirement of an independent board of directors should be sufficient to protect corporate colleges from being financially exploited by their parent companies.

4. In this case, the court held that it was not unreasonable for accrediting associations to refuse to evaluate proprietary institutions on the grounds that the profit motive could interfere with the educational program.

Curriculum. One concern expressed about corporate education is that it teaches students only those courses needed to perform a specific job and has no liberal education component. This concern, however, should argue for the careful evaluation by accreditors of the curriculum of corporate colleges rather than against all corporate education, or even all corporate colleges.

The states' alternatives

An earlier section reported the results of a survey of state higher education associations and the three basic approaches states use when they receive applications for degree-granting authority from noneducational entities (see table 2). This section explains these approaches in more detail.

Approach one: Ignore the problem. Given the limited financial resources of many states and the growing antigovernment mood of many voters, it has become clear that government should regulate only when a problem occurs or is likely to occur. One state official in this study commented that there has been no need to set policy because no corporation or professional association has ever made a request. If a state waits too long, however, it will be more difficult—even impossible—to regulate the situation effectively.

A state with essentially no degree-granting authority of its own might suggest to its institutions that they alert their accrediting associations to the situation so that the association can study the situation if it has not already done so. And a state might discuss with its educational institutions the reasons that corporate colleges are being established to give institutions some lead time in meeting the needs of the corporate sector.

Approach two: Treat noncollegiate-sponsored institutions as private institutions. This approach is by far the most common among the states. The obvious advantage of this approach is that it treats everyone the same. Noncollegiate institutions will be neither aided nor penalized by special regulations, and questions of equity aside, due process may require this approach.

This approach also assumes that noncollegiate institutions are the same as collegiate institutions. Three states responding that they will treat noncollegiate institutions like private institutions indicated that they would first require the institutions to comply with the state law governing nonprofit corporations, although they did not say that institutional board members cannot also be corporation board members. While it is still possible for the institutional board to be controlled by the corporate board (particularly if the membership is identical), separate incorporation does help eliminate the problem of financial decisions being made for reasons that favor the corporation over the corporate college.

Approach three: Require an independent board of directors for the corporate college (the Massachusetts approach). The Massachusetts approach deserves special consideration because Massachusetts has faced this situation more recently and more frequently than any other state.

Massachusetts requires that corporate colleges have an independent board of directors [604 CMR 11.03(3)(a)(3), (4)]. It does not define "independent," but it would seem to imply that at least a majority of the institutional board members are not also members of the corporation's board. This situation would prevent both financial control and excessive corporate influence, both of which could seriously impinge upon academic freedom. An additional advantage of the Massachusetts approach is that it will help to protect academic freedom for faculty and students. Faculty members in corporate colleges need at least as much protection to teach and conduct research freely as faculty members in other types of colleges. An independent board could help insulate them from potential political pressure from corporate officials.

This approach provides some assurance that a corporation that is willing to set up an independent board is genuinely interested in education for qualified students and not a narrow form of training for a restricted student body. Students enrolled in an accredited institution are eligible for federal financial aid, and if institutions have unreasonably restrictive entrance requirements (employment in the sponsoring firm, for example), the use of federal monies could become controversial.

Several arguments exist for continuing to grant legitimate recognition to corporate colleges. American higher education has thrived on diversity, and a movement to standardize higher education would be counterproductive. Corporations claim that their education is distinctive in offering more individualized instruction at a time and location convenient to students. It may also be pedagogically sound to link education and work (Cross 1981), theory and practice, as the community colleges have.

Accrediting body approaches
Regional and other institutional accrediting associations have long had a policy of judging a college in terms of what it pur-

ports to do; this policy does not give them much ground for refusing to accredit corporate colleges, even if they were inclined to do so. Eight corporate colleges have received institutional accreditation from the regional associations, and six other colleges with degree-granting authority are now in various stages of applying for accreditation. Two of the corporate colleges, GMI and the Boston Architectural Center, have received specialized program accreditation.

Many corporate programs cannot meet the current standards established by the appropriate program recognizers relating to admissions, faculty, and campus environment. The stated policy of the regional accreditation associations is to evaluate how well an institution meets its mission. The missions of corporate colleges, however, may well be different from more traditional institutions. Such missions might also be inconsistent with some of the standards currently used by the accrediting associations. Thus, the accreditation associations might develop new standards for evaluating corporate colleges, even though doing so could prove costly, time consuming, and appropriately controversial.

Another concern is academic freedom. Traditionally, education is considered most valuable when academic freedom is preserved. Many companies have not adequately provided for this assurance, however, and accrediting associations need to account for the protection of academic freedom when assessing a corporate college.

Alternatively, many reasons have been advanced why a recognizing association would want to react favorably to corporate colleges. Agencies committed to promoting and ensuring high quality in education will want to consider all education, not only traditional forms. Further, an agency's expertise in the evaluation of educational quality could help corporations improve the quality of programs. Ignoring these opportunities may not be consistent with the agency's goals.

The variety among specialized accrediting agencies extends to purpose, standards, content, nomenclature, format, style, and institutional types (Peterson 1979). Therefore, several approaches are available for responding to applications for accreditation. The following analysis assists in determining a response for any particular specialized agency.

The possible combinations of institutions and programs can be categorized in four ways:

- traditional institution–traditional program
- nontraditional institution–traditional program
- traditional institution–nontraditional program
- nontraditional institution–nontraditional program.

A traditional institution is a nonprofit college or university; a traditional program is one that has existed for some time and has been adopted by many other institutions. The majority of specialized accrediting institutions respond mostly to this combination but have also formulated a statement of how they will apply standards to the second and third categories above.

The interesting feature of current programs at corporate colleges is that many corporate colleges offer not only a nontraditional program (class scheduling, opportunity for applied practice for credit, faculty expertise and credentials) but also a unique service, which places them in the fourth category. Yet few specialized accreditors respond directly to the problem of accrediting nontraditional programs at nontraditional institutions, and therein lies the problem. The approaches available to these agencies range from continuing to ignore these entities to adopting new standards for accreditation. Ignoring the problem could lead the growing number of nontraditional institutions to seek accreditation elsewhere, even by starting their own organization.

The Council on Postsecondary Accreditation (1981) recommends that the same standards for similar programs should apply to traditional and nontraditional institutions, because problems could arise if nontraditional members had to meet stricter standards to obtain the same accreditation. Separate standards for new nontraditional programs could be developed, however. Different associations could also develop their own approaches.[5] A recommended response for specialized agencies is to determine which new programs (at either traditional or nontraditional institutions) are developing to the point where it would be cost beneficial to establish new standards for those programs. The effort will require cooperating with other institutional accrediting agencies, with nontraditional institutions with established programs (or the developing programs), and with other specialized agencies reviewing other programs or with an interest in the programs.

5. The Southern Association and the North Central Association differ as to how to accredit two-year institutions.

Much of this discussion leads one to consider what the education community might expect from corporate education in the future. The next section examines the factors that affect the development of corporate education and possible responses of the formal recognizing associations.

The Future of Corporate Education

Several reasons are apparent for the expansion of education offered by employers to employees, and each is likely to continue to be a potent factor throughout the remainder of the twentieth century.

Technology

Perhaps the biggest factor affecting the growth of corporate education today is the growth of technology. Changing technology leads to job changes as current work is taken over by machines, creating new kinds of work, and employees need to be educated to make those changes.

In response to technological change, corporations will continue to educate not only those employees whose work is altered by the technology but also those who develop it. Much research is done in corporate laboratories, and many companies are on the leading edge of technology. In a highly competitive environment, firms are not inclined to share their proprietary knowledge with outsiders, even for training purposes.

Demographics

Unlike the rest of our history, where each generation was larger than its predecessor, the current generation in high school and college is notably smaller than previous generations. This fact has several implications for corporate education.

The work force in the United States is aging and cannot be readily replenished. Concurrently, people are healthier and can work longer, when company policies allow. Therefore, that older work force will need to be retrained to deal with the rapid change in technology. And that retraining will consist of programs or courses geared to a specific need.

When baby boomers reach retirement age, an unusually large proportion of the population will leave the work force within a very short amount of time. They will need to be replaced, and competition for workers will be strong. Corporations may well compete with colleges for young people, offering them education and the opportunity for a career at the same time. The combination of technological innovation and demographic change has led to smaller numbers of prepared workers for the jobs of the future. Corporations necessarily had to step in to train workers because they could not afford to wait for the education sector to train them. And the pattern is likely to be repeated.

Perhaps the biggest factor affecting the growth of corporate education today is the growth of technology.

Cost effectiveness

Corporations are finding that it is more cost effective to "make" education than to "buy" it. Corporations need to do a certain amount of training because no one else is available or willing to do it, but once corporations have established a training program, the cost of adding another course becomes marginal, less than the full cost. This observation is especially true of the large companies, which have extensive education and training centers (and spend the most money on education).

With their own courses, companies can tailor the curriculum so that it meets their needs, thereby saving time and money. If a corporation wants its engineers and salesmen to learn a foreign language so that the company can do business in a country where that language is spoken, it will want employees to learn a different vocabulary from that normally taught in an introductory language class. They save time and money by designing their own courses. Furthermore, it is costly to negotiate with another organization, and when a corporation has the educational structure in place, it may not be worth its time to work with a university to design the educational programs the corporation desires.

Self-declared intent to expand

Corporations have declared their intent to expand—or at least to maintain—their educational activities (Lusterman 1985; Pitre 1980). They intend to expand first those activities over which they have the most control and least contact with the outside (in-house courses) and last those activities over which they have the least control and most outside contact (college credit).

Promotion from within

Many corporations are committed, by policy or union contract, to promotion from within. This policy saves the costs of orientation and of the lag time during which workers adjust to a new company. Many corporations also think that promotion from within builds loyalty and morale. For companies to promote employees, however, they often need to train workers for the next level of responsibility.

Dissatisfaction with colleges and universities

Theoretically, corporations could buy much of the education they need from colleges and universities. For a variety of reasons, however, it is unlikely to happen.

Higher education has historically been reluctant to provide "practical" training, generally seeing its purpose as that of providing an education, not a narrow form of training (although community colleges are a notable departure from that philosophy). Even when colleges and universities do train an individual for a career, a strong liberal arts component is almost always included. Indeed, the pendulum has swung in recent years toward a greater liberal arts component. It is not necessary to take sides in the debate to realize that this trend will be unacceptable to some individuals and some corporations.

More important, however, is that corporations have found colleges and universities rigid and uncooperative (Cross 1981; Goldstein 1980; Lynton 1981, 1984). Higher education heretofore has been inflexible in a number of areas, although recent initiatives in the form of corporate education centers, designed to address special, employer-specific training needs (Eastern Michigan University's Corporate Management Education Center and the University of Toledo's Seagate Center, for example) may mitigate this factor.

Many colleges and universities are reluctant or unable to envision, much less offer, a course that does not meet the college's standard time schedule. Colleges often find it difficult to offer a course that is a month shorter, or longer, or more intensive, than the standard course. It is not only that colleges have legitimate questions about the number of credits that a shortened course should have, it is that colleges are also unwilling or unable to provide it. Many colleges and universities also refuse to offer courses on a corporate worksite open only to corporate employees.

Although this situation is less true now than it was, many colleges do not understand the need of adult students to work and therefore to enroll in part-time programs. This problem is especially prevalent at the graduate level, where residency requirements are still common.

Corporations sometimes wish to provide their own instructors for courses and receive college credit for doing so. Although some colleges are willing to agree to such arrangements, particularly in small communities where the individuals with the most expertise in a subject work for the corporation, more often colleges refuse to consider such arrangements. Certainly, colleges have an obligation to guarantee the quality of their faculty. Too often, however, colleges refuse to let an individual teach because that individual does not have a doctorate, even if the individual is on the leading edge in his or her field. Like refusing to offer a six-month rather than a four-month course, this situation can elevate form over substance.

Two of the most serious criticisms corporations direct at higher education concern course offerings. Unlike some of the other criticisms, which involve only some cosmetic changes in a college's operations, these two go to the heart of the missions of colleges and universities.

Corporations charge that higher education sometimes will not offer courses in subject matters of interest to them. For example, a large chemical company in a northern state noted that the state university 40 miles away would not offer courses in polymers, which would attract a fairly steady demand from corporate employees, because the professoriate was not interested in the subject and did not consider it part of the university's mission. Instead, the company offered the courses and the university granted credit. The company was content with the arrangement and had no intention of creating a degree-granting institution. Colleges are, of course, free to offer what they choose. If they choose not to offer courses needed by corporations, however, they should not be surprised when the corporations offer the courses themselves.

The second criticism about courses is that colleges do not train students well to adjust to the world of work—specifically, that students do not know how to work in groups. Higher education's emphasis on individual achievement and on competition with little attention to group efforts does not prepare students for the real world of committee decisions.

Finally, corporations complain that colleges move too slowly. College procedures generally hinder the addition of courses in a short period of time. Once a corporation has gone through its own procedures to determine the need for a course, additional delay to meet collegiate practices and policies is often unacceptable to the corporation.

What often happens is that the corporation bypasses the college and hires the professor directly. The corporation may then get the course evaluated for credit, and the college may end up granting credit for it after all. Meanwhile, the college has lost money and, more important, good will with a neighboring business.

Continued Recognition of Corporate Education
Even granting that corporate education will continue to grow, does it necessarily mean that corporations will continue to seek

recognition for their educational efforts? All indications are that the answer to this question is also "yes."

Underlying this discussion is the assumption that this society is increasingly credential conscious. More and more occupations are attempting to develop educational requirements and accrediting organizations and to have them accepted as mandatory by state governments (Coordinating Board 1980). Although something of a backlash has developed to the push for increasingly stringent educational requirements and the proliferation of accrediting agencies, the history of accreditation shows a tendency toward more rather than less regulation. If this tendency continues, corporations will of course see that their employees get the credentials they need.

Employees prefer to attend courses that have been recognized. Of 39 organizations whose courses had been evaluated by ACE or the New York Regents, more than half reported that since evaluation, enrollment in the courses increased and students' performance improved (Pitre 1980). Further, credit is a relatively inexpensive fringe benefit. If employees want it and it will improve their educational effort, corporations will provide credentials. And many employees enrolled in corporate credit-bearing courses eventually seek degrees in colleges and universities, increasing their usefulness to the employer and, incidentally, increasing college enrollment.

Corporations take great pride in the quality of their educational offerings. They want to have their courses recognized as the equivalent of college courses. With the availability of the ACE and New York Regents evaluation programs, it is not prohibitively expensive for corporations to have their courses evaluated, not only providing a form of quality control for them, but also giving them an opportunity to advertise to their employees and to the outside world that their education is comparable to that of colleges and universities.

Corporations might not go through the steps of receiving recognition and degree-granting authority if those steps were difficult or time consuming. As many corporations have discovered, however, formal recognition is not that hard to get. It is true that most states have rigorous requirements for institutions to grant degrees; institutions must receive approval from a state higher education agency, which sets requirements in terms of necessary capital, professors, curriculum, and so on. Some states, of course, have virtually no requirements to become a degree-granting institution—the only things needed are three incorporators and $500. The number of courses evaluated favorably by ACE and the New York Regents and the number of corporate colleges incorporated in states with rigorous requirements indicate that corporations will not have a problem achieving recognition of their programs.

Therefore, one can expect that corporations will continue to provide their employees with continuing education. The intellectual stimulation, the opportunity for career advancement, and the opportunity such work affords the company to stimulate corporate loyalty and attract and retain the kind of employees the firm desires can all be expected to justify large expenditures for corporate education.

In many ways, colleges helped to create the continuing need for education of employees by expanding the intellectual horizons of more and more students who continue, as adults, to seek knowledge and intellectual stimulation and by creating knowledge that should be disseminated so that adults benefit from seeking such knowledge. An employer, recognizing this curiosity and need to be informed, appropriately seeks to provide to some extent some means by which employees can fulfill their need to know. Because many employees are overeducated for the work they do and need to find personal satisfaction beyond their work and responsibilities, a firm may be able to retain employees by meeting their needs in a more complete way (O'Toole 1978).

The Posture of Formal Recognizers
This section outlines issues that different members of the collegiate community might want to consider as corporate education grows and diversifies.

Accrediting associations
The United States has always been able to accommodate diverse institutions of higher education and should be able to assimilate corporate education. By considering corporate education in the mainstream of education, accrediting associations will discourage corporate educators from forming their own accrediting association. Such an association would further isolate corporate education and prevent corporate and collegiate educators from learning from one another. To the extent that businesses provide credit-bearing education instead of company courses, they hold the same public trust that higher education

holds. Thus, their courses must have an applicability beyond a specific skill needed by a specific company at a specific time. If the standards used for educational organizations meet the criteria set by accreditors for accepting or approving applications, any applicant should have to meet the same standards.

Although accrediting associations claim to evaluate colleges and programs on how well they meet their stated purposes, in fact only a small proportion of their accrediting standards speak directly to that issue. If, for example, a nursing school claimed that it trains students to practice as nurses—that is, to pass the state nursing examination—the only factor the National League of Nursing would need to evaluate would be the success rate of nursing graduates on the state examination. The same could be said for the graduates of other professional programs like law and medicine. Instead, of course, the passage rate is only one of the measures of quality accrediting associations use.

The essential question—and the one that remains unanswered—is whether or not the standards set are sufficient to ensure some degree of quality. The focus of the accreditation standards is on internal institutional factors—education of the faculty, library holdings, financial viability, for example. With occasional discontent, colleges and universities have accepted these proxy standards for students' learning because they too believe that a relationship exists between the percentage of the professoriate with a doctoral degree and students' learning. Possible criteria for accreditation can include assessing performance of an educational institution on the basis of outcomes like graduates' performance on standardized tests, the rates at which students secure jobs or enroll in graduate school, and the quality of postbaccalaureate performance at work or in graduate school. The commendable focus on quality recommended by the COPA self-study advisory committee will add further credence to accreditation in a substantially diversified marketplace (COPA 1986). Nevertheless, data on such variables are limited and costly to gather and maintain.

The core of the discussion of the formal recognition of corporate or other nontraditional sponsored instruction is the assurance of quality to the public. Toward that end, it is essential to move beyond narrow and mechanistic criteria and explore the activities, strategies, and behavior accrediting associations use to ensure that they serve to improve the services of accredited institutions and programs (COPA 1986). The responsibility continues to be diffused throughout the education establishment, including institutions, private and public agencies, and accrediting and professional associations.

Collegiate institutions

The traditional exchange of credits among institutions historically has been among comparable institutions, but the situation is changing as more and more corporate courses earn credits and more and more colleges approve such credits toward their own degrees. Whenever an institution accepts previous coursework for credit, it is in effect losing tuition income from students who have paid for those outside credits elsewhere.

One can argue, as some corporations are suggesting, that many employees who take credit-bearing courses at the plant continue to work toward degrees at colleges and universities—degrees that they might not have sought without the impetus of credit from corporate courses. That case represents an increase in enrollment for the colleges.

The mixture of coursework from different sources can be a problem in quality in the sense that students' overall programs may lack coherence and consistency. While accreditation groups that approve such coursework ostensibly are expected to ensure some consistency across institutions in comparable coursework, accreditation for individual courses and overall program and institutional accreditation conducted on different levels and by different organizations raise concern about consistency and coherence—and quality.

A recent report (Mortimer 1984) suggests that colleges specify what minimum competencies students should have to receive a baccalaureate degree and then develop evaluation tools that can measure whether students have achieved those competencies. This recommendation has particular cogency for corporate education. It may be that education received by a full-time student in a liberal arts college differs from education received by a part-time student at work. If higher education cannot state what it means to have a baccalaureate degree and how it knows when a student has earned one, it is not in a position to argue the distinction with any confidence, however. Similarly, accrediting associations, which have set minimum standards, may want to reexamine their position, although one could argue that the marketplace will maintain or close institutions on the basis of fiscal and reputational recognition and that legal recognition plays a different role.

Agencies that confer degree-granting authority

Just as colleges and universities need to decide what a baccalaureate degree means, state agencies need to decide what it means to be a degree-granting institution. Some states have no requirements at all for persons wishing to form degree-granting institutions. Other states have requirements and enforce them but have not thought about the issue of corporate colleges. State degree-granting agencies and the regional accrediting bodies might follow the lead of the Massachusetts Board of Higher Education and ensure that the boards of corporate colleges are independent from the sponsoring corporations. If corporations apply for credit evaluation from a group like the New York Regents or the American Council on Education, that group should encourage its own instructors to exercise academic freedom.

State higher education agencies

With the advent of the 1202 commissions, mandated by the federal government for the purpose of planning postsecondary education, including proprietary institutions, states were enjoined to consider all of postsecondary education in their planning. Most states do not consider corporate education, however, for two reasons. Higher education agencies generally do not know enough about corporate education in their states to do any planning with them in mind. Some state agencies—departments of labor or employee relations, for example—might know a great deal about some types of corporate training, particularly those for which state or federal funds are given, but they are likely to talk about educational efforts only when they compete for the right to administer funds, such as those from the Job Training Partnership Act.

State higher education agencies need not attempt to control, or even plan for, corporate education, except insofar as corporate education attempts to confer credits or degrees. Higher education agencies—especially state agencies with responsibility for community colleges—should take corporate education into account when planning for education, however.[6]

State higher education policies should not undermine successful corporate educational programs. Including corporate education managers with corporate executives in discussions of postsecondary education will promote a cooperative planning

6. Some proprietary schools view corporate education as a greater source of competition than the community colleges.

atmosphere. Such cooperation will also assist in ensuring that accurate and complete information about all postsecondary education delivery systems is made available to states and other comprehensive planners.

Fiscal Implications

Formal and informal recognition of instruction has fiscal implications because of the direction of federal student aid funds and the funneling of other federal dollars to bona fide educational establishments. They vary with regard to any specifications regarding degree-granting authority and/or accreditation on a given piece of legislation. The legitimacy of an educational institution also affects the selection of individuals who use their own money to purchase an education.

As a rule, however, corporate education courses and programs are funded by employers, either those offering instruction for their own employees or those sending their employees to programs sponsored by other corporations. In that sense, the growth in the number of recognized courses is not a public issue, as allocations of those funds are private decisions.

The question arises, however, whether or not public funds should be invested in private educational programs like the corporate education programs discussed here. Some might say that because education is a cost of doing business, like any other business expense it should be borne exclusively by the business firm. Society's educational role lies in the obligation to provide a literate, educated citizenry. It is not necessarily society's obligation to provide workers with narrow skills at the taxpayers' expense. Colleges will be stronger if they are not so strongly driven by erratic vocational demands.

Another argument is that government has a role to educate a competent work force adaptable to changes in demographics, technology, and the balance of foreign trade. Therefore, government should support education without undue regard for the provider so long as some assurance is available that the provider can do so adequately. In fact, the federal government has provided funds for training conducted by business and industry with special attention to such training in the Job Training Partnership Act.

An array of proposed federal bills addresses this question through the tax code or other indirect or direct subsidies to American businesses to provide education for employees. If these proposed pieces of legislation are adopted, the need will be great to study the impact on both workers and educational delivery systems.

Still, in light of this discussion, it is important to keep in mind that corporate colleges can only be regarded like any other collegiate institution, because in every way, except perhaps for the motives under which they were founded, they are legitimate, formally recognized postsecondary institutions.

Summary and Conclusions

Corporate education has grown in size, content, and sophistication since its inception in the days of apprenticeship schools. In the early twentieth century, corporations were indifferent to or contemptuous of college degrees, and the nature of much corporate education was company specific, short term, and ad hoc. The question of credit for corporate education did not arise. In recent years, however, academic credentials have become more important. The New York Regents and the American Council on Education began to evaluate corporate education and recommend college credit. Some corporations went even further, founding their own degree-granting colleges.

All indications are that corporate education will continue to grow in the future. The factors leading to the growth of corporate education, primarily demographics and technology, will continue to be important. Corporations need to have a work force able to perform the kinds of work the firms require to remain viable and profitable. As long as companies are satisfied with their own delivery systems, they can be expected to maintain and even to develop them.

Colleges have traditionally shown a reluctance to become involved in practical education. "Functional" education took a giant leap forward after World War II with the formation of community colleges.[7] While some colleges are interested in cooperating with corporations in providing education to corporate workers, many are not. Sometimes practical difficulties prevent even the most willing college/corporate ventures from being successful, however.

7. Technical institutes were ahead of community colleges in this area, as the early community colleges emphasized transfer education over occupational training. In the 1960s, community colleges entered the arena of technical institutes.

Higher education needs to acknowledge the existence and legitimacy of corporate education. Having done that, higher education needs to ensure that corporate education meets high standards of quality, which can be accomplished through normal recognition processes. State degree-granting agencies and accreditation agencies are equipped to evaluate corporate education. The question of standards set for recognition is stimulated by the entrance of corporations into the collegiate environment.

IMPLICATIONS OF EXPANDING RECOGNIZED CORPORATE EDUCATION

What does this growth of formally recognized education in noncollegiate settings mean to the new deliverers of such education (the corporations and businesses), the traditional deliverers (colleges and universities), the organizations that confer recognition, and the recipients of such education?

Before pursuing that discussion, it is appropriate to note that all corporate education is in no way to be viewed as postsecondary education, particularly with regard to company-specific information that is not transferable to other places of employment.

Some gray areas exist, however. One such area is skill building, because community colleges and technical schools, long since considered postsecondary education, provide much that is similar. Another poorly defined area is remedial or basic education. In part, the need to provide remedial education to adult workers is an indictment of education through grade 12 in this country and is a problem shared jointly by traditional postsecondary education institutions and corporate education organizations. In another sense, it is a reflection of changing demands in the workplace that now require more sophistication for newly created and designed jobs. Basic skills long unused need to be renewed.

In part, the need to provide remedial education to adult workers is an indictment of education through grade 12 in this country.

Employers as Educators

All indications are that business and industry are deeply committed to maintaining and expanding their workers at all levels in the enterprise. Their alternatives are, as noted earlier, to buy such training from postsecondary education institutions, to buy it from consulting firms or individual trainers, and/or to offer education and training themselves. As philosophies of human resource development change, as the business climate changes, as technology and demographics affect business and industry, so will their attention to education be modified.

The most important reason for employers' educating their employees is to obtain and maintain a competitive edge in the marketplace. An obvious aspect of the education of workers is the assurance that participants in the programs not only learn what is taught but also can translate the information into behavior once back at work (Hawthorne *forthcoming*). When corporations control education for their employees, they have a better opportunity to facilitate the transition between classroom and office or factory, because they can adapt the education and the worksite in a coordinated manner if they choose to. For this purpose, employers' continued delivery of education is desirable. It is not unreasonable to assume, however, that once corporate educators vigorously link education with the worksite, the task could be accomplished in concert with a compatible college or university.

Pricing policies in postsecondary education can also serve to affect choices made by employers in identifying preferred options for educating their employees. As the fiscal position of individual businesses or whole industries ebb and flow, their willingness and ability to allocate resources to education will affect the choices of delivery systems.

Traditional Postsecondary Education Institutions

Higher education in the United States has consistently, albeit sometimes reluctantly, responded to changing opportunities in the workplace with the addition of courses, programs, and advanced degrees. This adaptability has been the hallmark of American higher education (Ben-David 1972).

The proliferation of corporate education in general, and of formally recognized corporate education specifically, has given educators an opportunity to examine the direction and purposes of postsecondary education in terms of who is in fact providing postsecondary instruction and who *should* provide it. One area in which colleges and universities can fill a need is in the provision of training and education, whether for credit or not, for employees of small businesses who cannot provide their own instruction. Many firms are not large enough to develop educational programs but have needs similar to those of larger corporations. This area necessitates vigorous outreach and an assessment of need by community colleges, colleges, and universities.

Furthermore, the passage of legislation under consideration by Congress to direct federal funds to corporations for training and retraining workers could be at considerable cost to colleges and universities. It behooves college and university administrators to be informed about the progress of these bills and to build relationships with corporations that will facilitate a partnership to the use of these monies.

Probably the most pressing consideration for traditional collegiate institutions has to do with the transfer of credit from one educational program, from one institution, to another. In many cases, students will ask for credit from diverse sources of instruction. It becomes eminently clear that actors from all segments of postsecondary education should begin to regard one another as colleagues, not competitors, to facilitate education for learners.

Formal Recognizers of Postsecondary Education
Formal recognizers have gone great distances to bring corporate education into the mainstream of postsecondary education in the United States. Having done so, recognizers should endeavor to maintain consistency in the application of their standards to education and training, without regard to the type of sponsor (Harcleroad 1980, pp. 35–36). As long as the same organizations recognize individuals, courses, programs, and institutions using the same standards for all those reviewed, there is little reason to be concerned that the new entrant on the scene will have a negative impact on the quality of education.

The founding of corporate colleges has some implications for state agencies. Major corporations may establish corporate colleges in one state and may desire at a future date to expand their degree-granting opportunities to employees in other states. Such institutions, called "foreign" institutions, are those that have degree-granting authority in one state and begin to offer courses in or establish a campus in another state, without having gone through the second state's degree-granting approval process.

Colleges are able to do so in many states because those states allow any college with degree-granting authority in another state that is accredited by a regional association to receive degree-granting authority within that state. As shown in table 3, some states have virtually no laws governing the award of degree-granting authority (although the number of such states has declined in recent years). It is for this reason that states have added the proviso that the colleges also have regional accreditation, leading to criticisms from some states that the accrediting associations are not strict enough in monitoring colleges for quality (Ashworth 1979) and responses from accrediting associations that protecting states from foreign institutions is not their purpose (Young 1983).

Accreditation, while legally optional, has been growing in its importance because of the value assigned to formal credentials by our highly mobile society, a society of strangers very dependent on objective standards by which to select desirable affiliations. The degree to which an institution can choose not to volunteer to apply for and be granted accreditation is essentially nonexistent. Indeed, in *Majorie Webster* v. *Middle States Association*, the lower court (subsequently overturned) found that the Middle States Association could not refuse to review the proprietary school's application for accreditation because of its proprietary nature, because accreditation is so important to an institution that it is no longer actually a voluntary act. The importance of accreditation by regional associations is highlighted in the example of the Swain School of Design. A 100-year-old college of art, the school applied for accreditation by the New England Association of Schools and Colleges because the faculty thought it would "help the school attract funds and students and [because it was] a matter of professional pride" (*Chronicle of Higher Education* 3 February 1982, p. 3). The school had already been accredited by the National Association of Schools of Art and Design.

Finally, it has been argued, the issue of public trust in accreditation implies the need to broaden the input into accreditation, because the anonymity of accrediting people allows for no checks and balances, which is a hallmark of our system of government (Dickey and Miller 1972, p. 28; see also Harcleroad 1980 and Orlans 1975). Today, it is appropriate for accrediting associations to broaden the scope of their membership to include representatives from corporate education facilities, which would additionally serve to avoid the proliferation of accrediting associations.

Recipients of Postsecondary Education
Corporations eager for highly skilled workers may be willing to recruit them directly from high school and ensure them of a paid college education on the corporate campus while working and earning a salary. This scenario is quite likely, given the precipitous drop in the number of high school graduates at a time when many older workers are retiring.

Toward Coordination
The challenge before us is not to decide who will deliver education but "how to develop a synergistic, positive relationship between the academy and the corporation. . . (Morse 1984, p. 63). This statement should be of assurance to traditional educators concerned that the growth of corporate education represents a threat to their institutions' vitality.

Colleges and universities have developed initiatives to aid business and industry in their quest for skilled employees at all levels. Greatly expanded continuing education programs and sophisticated marketing approaches are moving colleges and universities into coordinated efforts with business, each building on its own expertise to meet what can easily be viewed as needs of society. These efforts by colleges and universities also suggest that academics are learning to speak the language of business, a factor that most certainly contributes to greater facility in communication and bodes well for the future.

Another collegiate initiative is a modification of the continuing education divisions added to college campuses. Such corporate education centers often exist side by side with divisions of continuing education. In some cases, either or both arrange programs in which some courses are taught at the institution and some at the sponsoring corporation. Through such organizational structures, many colleges "customize" their courses for interested corporations.

These centers and other administrative arrangements offer contract courses—courses offered by a college for a specific corporation and usually, although not always, taught by college faculty members. The corporations recruit and select the employees, pay them, and provide administrative assistance and facilities. The college charges tuition and may also charge an administrative fee. This arrangement is a useful one for larger corporations. The colleges award a variety of "certifications," including academic credits, degrees, occupational certification, CEUs, and "documentation of satisfactory performance." The most common is academic credit (College Entrance Examination Board 1984).

Colleges and universities offer both credit and noncredit courses to corporations as well as jointly sponsor degree programs with them. A study of 2,623 institutions found that almost half of them offered credit courses (47 percent) and noncredit courses (48 percent). Nineteen percent offered jointly sponsored degree programs (El-Khawas 1984).

The numbers vary by type of institution. Fifty-nine percent of two-year colleges, 26 percent of baccalaureate colleges, and 49 percent of universities offer credit courses, while virtually the same percentages offer noncredit courses. Twenty-six percent of two-year colleges, 9 percent of baccalaureate colleges, and 17 percent of universities sponsor joint degree programs (El-Khawas 1984).

Examples of joint educational ventures by corporations and colleges abound. Employees of Motorola in Phoenix, Arizona, for example, can earn an associate degree from Rio Salado Community College through contract courses. The University System of New Hampshire offers courses in computer studies (statistics, computer literacy, BASIC, COBOL, PASCAL, and FORTRAN) as well as courses in general studies at Data General. Worcester State College offers Conversational French for Programmers at the Norton Company, for which employees can receive three hours of credit (College Entrance Examination Board 1984).

Other corporations and colleges have other types of cooperative arrangements—Carnegie-Mellon and the Westinghouse Electric Robotics Institution, and the MIT and IBM and Digital Equipment computer programs, for example (Douglas 1984). In a more general way, colleges can capture the corporate education market by customizing coursework for specific corporate clients (Luther 1984).

On the other hand, we can expect business and industry to develop their own training to serve special needs. One major educational initiative has been jointly undertaken by the United Auto Workers and General Motors. The potential student body numbers 40,000 students and has been developed with extensive programming but no formal credit. Employees seeking advanced degrees or other forms of credit may take advantage of the tuition reimbursement plan, which has been improved to facilitate employees' use of it (Sorge 1986, p. 1c).

Evidence suggests that corporate education actually encourages students to enroll in colleges and universities (McQuigg 1980). In this respect, corporate education provides a stimulus to traditional higher education. Because of the growing kinship between corporate education and collegiate education, both sectors could work together to integrate courses and programs, serving to reduce overlap and to facilitate transfers.

OPPORTUNITIES FOR RESEARCH

Fiscal Aspects of the Corporate Education "Phenomenon"

The implications of the emergence of corporate education into postsecondary education for the economic viability of traditional postsecondary education is not well understood. A major stumbling block to this understanding is the variation in cost accounting for training in business and industry and the proprietary nature of those figures, making many firms reluctant to release the information. Related is the need for more information on the extent of corporate education: what it is, how much it costs, who gets it, and what good it does. Some standard definitions of terms could facilitate this research—for example, what is meant by "management education," "functional-technical education," "white-collar training."

Public policy issues of who pays for education for work requires much more investigation (Lynton 1984), particularly in light of federal investment in the education of workers. If more and more education is provided by employers without charge to employees, the general public pays in the marketplace and may pay again if the education the corporation provides is a tax credit for the firm. Publicly supported education obviously costs every taxpayer, but what are the alternative arguments and issues in regard to the questions of "who pays" and "who should pay"?

If more and more education is provided by employers without charge to employees, the general public pays in the marketplace and may pay again if the education . . . is a tax credit for the firm.

Internal Studies of Corporate Education

Educators from both colleges and corporations would benefit from more thorough scrutiny of corporate college curricula, their organization and content, who the faculty are and where they come from, and the numbers and types of students they serve with regard to their demographic, educational, and employment backgrounds before entering corporate colleges.

Similarly, studies would be helpful comparing graduates of corporate colleges and traditional colleges. Such studies should measure work-related factors like job satisfaction and advancement, salaries, and career changes and personal factors like continued education for personal and professional development and what may loosely be described as "life satisfaction."

Longitudinal studies need to be developed of the effectiveness of education in the corporation with regard to workers' and the firm's productivity. Such research would also have implications for research on outcomes of traditional educational institutions and courses and consequently for accreditation and other forms of formal recognition.

Corporations are inconsistent in matching employees with certain courses. Research on the relationship between students' characteristics in a corporate setting and the courses with regard to techniques of instruction and benefits to the individual and to the firm would go a long way toward making education more cost effective. Such research should include follow-up studies of the retention of students in corporate education programs and their career paths.

Continued study of the dynamics of instructional technology in different environments to achieve different pedagogical objectives would contribute greatly to the growing literature on both cost-benefit analysis of instructional technology (Kearsley 1982) and on teaching and learning in higher education. (The reader is referred to the National Center on Research on Postsecondary Teaching and Learning at the University of Michigan for more information in this critical area.)

The Role of Education in Organizational Change

It is not well understood what role education plays in organizational change. Many factors cause change in an organization—for example, shifts of personnel, changes in corporate policy, new products, and acquisitions. And while education is often systematically designed to cause change, it is not known whether education is more suited to certain kinds of change under specified conditions. Do opportunities exist to combine education with, say, policy changes that are designed to lead toward specified changes within the organization? Because evaluation in corporate education does not often relate the outcomes of the training to the specific problems the training was supposed to affect, the dynamics of training as it affects performance are less well understood than firms would like.

Alternative Routes for Education of Employees

Considerable informal, on-the-job training is available for workers in all reported occupations (Carnevale 1986, p. 19). On-the-job training can be costly to employers for the time of the trainee and the trainee's fellow workers, whose work time is distracted by the investment in training. It is likely that a systematic examination of the content and nature of this training may be helpful in identifying pretraining opportunities that can be provided in a more cost-effective manner. Research of this kind can readily be conducted jointly by academics and corporate educators.

Substantive published research is apparently not available concerning the alternative routes for corporations to take in providing educational opportunities for their employees. For example, if a corporation were to institute some educational program, what would the costs and benefits be of establishing a corporate college or a corporate education center with or without credit-bearing courses, of developing opportunities in conjunction with traditional colleges and universities, or of reimbursing employees for tuition?

Similarly, little sound evidence is available to guide decision making in colleges and universities regarding the organizational structure most conducive to the provision of services to business and industry. Some campuses provide dual structures, such as the presence of continuing education programs and corporate education centers. Related to this need is a better understanding of the relative effectiveness of different marketing strategies employed by colleges and universities to serve the training needs of business and industry.

Case Studies

Case studies of corporate education delivery systems and courses would be useful to other educators. They would also be helpful to those involved in the academic preparation of training specialists in business and industry. A systematic exploration of the beginnings and changes in corporate colleges in light of the relevance to traditional collegiate education is in order.

Proprietary Education

Proprietary education has failed to draw the attention of scholars. According to data from the National Center for Education Statistics (NCES), new part-time postsecondary education students are enrolling in private proprietary schools in growing proportions, even though the actual number of new part-time students has been declining since 1981. Because of the renewed and compelling interest in job training in both the private and the public sectors, the role of the proprietary schools, most commonly job training institutions, takes on particular importance in the discussion of emerging forces in postsecondary education.

Other data from NCES suggest its growing impact. Enrollments in private proprietary institutions accounted for 2.9 percent, 3 percent, 3.2 percent, 3.6 percent, and 6.1 percent of all full-time enrollments in two-year institutions from 1979 to 1984. Growth has been less dramatic for part-time students. With regard to baccalaureate-level enrollments, an area rarely associated historically with private proprietary institutions, the proprietary institutions are holding onto their market share in a declining market for both full-time and part-time students.

These data suggest that dynamics of the role of this segment of postsecondary education affect all aspects of postsecondary education that are not understood as well as the importance of increasing our knowledge about the dimensions of the development of proprietary schools—finances, enrollment, instruction, and changing methods of credentialing.

Recognition

Accreditation and other forms of formal recognition have developed out of a need for commonly understood standards amid a patchwork of educational enterprises. In some cases, standards establish stated minimum acceptable practices and procedures. In other instances, rigorous standards prevail, particularly in the professional fields of medicine and law. Much work remains to be done to develop methods for assessing the quality of education that includes both quantitative and qualitative approaches.

In this context, research into the public perception and acceptance of formal practices of recognition would enhance the postsecondary education community's efforts to improve recognition practices so as to improve the benefits that students derive from engaging in higher education, in whatever setting.

Education for Employment

Education for employment is a recurring theme in American higher education. Since the founding of Harvard College in 1636, American colleges and then universities in their own ways struggled with the challenges presented by a progressive, democratic society often offering unparalleled opportunities to its citizens. The challenge before American postsecondary education today—how to educate young people, middle-aged people, and older Americans for work and how to keep them attuned to the demands of the marketplace—requires intensive investigation. A particular consideration is the balance between liberal arts and humanities and between technical and professional education and training. Not only do we lack substantial data on this question; we also lack a national dialogue between educators and employers that will chart the courses that address the needs of students, colleges, and employers in some meaningful way.

The Whole Picture

These suggestions for research address pieces of the whole package of lifelong education for work, for leisure, and for enrichment provided by schools, colleges, professional associations, clubs, unions, and employers. While a "comprehensive analysis of the contributions and programs of the various providers" (Eurich 1985, p. 133) is needed, so too is a comprehensive analysis of learning needs as we move into the twenty-first century that will offer significant guidance in planning education—a process that should occur under the aegis of representatives from each of the teaching sectors. Competition—whether real or imagined—is not as likely to address the educational needs of adult Americans as are cooperation and a sense of shared purpose.

STATE LAWS ON DEGREE-GRANTING AND POSTSECONDARY INSTITUTIONS

State	Legislature Approves Colleges	Legislation Refers to a Higher Education Board	Legislation Excludes Accredited Colleges or Postsecondary Institutions[a]	Legislation Gives Guidance on Standards[b]	Only Nonprofit Corporation Language[c]	Statutory Authority
AL		Alabama State Department of Education (DOE)	Accrediting agency recognized by U.S. DOE, COPA, or Alabama State DOE			16§16-46-1 et seq.
AK		Alaska Commission on Postsecondary Education	Approved by Northwest Association or listed in Education Directory of U.S. Office of Education if Commission finds college acceptable; nonprofits excluded from requirements	X		§14.48.010 et seq.
AZ		State Board of Higher Education	Regional accreditors or temporary accreditation by Arizona			§10-1004
AR		State Board of Higher Education				80-4905
CA		Superintendent	DOE, Western Association, or Bar Examiners for the State of California, or approval for accreditation or licensure by State Board	X		§94302 et seq. Education Code
CO		Colorado Commission on Higher Education	Regional accreditors or a group determined by Colorado Commission to be acceptable			CRS 23-2-101
CT	Must be approved by General Assembly after review by State Board	Board of Governors	May accept national or regional accreditation			10a-34 et seq.

Appendix A (continued)

State	Agency	Description			Citation
DE					8§125
DC	State Board of Education Educational Institution Licensure Commission				§§31-1601 to 31-1608
FL	State Board of Independent Colleges and Universities	DOE, regional, or national accreditation or State Board + chartered in Florida or 3 letters from other colleges saying credits will be accepted			$246.011 et seq.
GA	State Board of Education	Accredited for more than 10 years	X		§20-3-100 et seq.
HI		Institution must state whether or not it is accredited[d]			25§§446E-1, 446E-2
ID	State DOE registers trade and correspondent schools	Regulates courses, excluding those offered by institution accredited by state or an agency recognized by state			33-2401 et seq.
IL	Board of Higher Education		X		144-121 et seq.
IN	Commission for Higher Education	Must be supported in whole or in part by state funds			§20-12-0.5-1 et seq.
IA			X	X	$504.10 et seq.
KS	Board of Regents	May be accepted by Regents	X		§74-3249 et seq.
KY	Council on Higher Education Board for Proprietary Education		X		KRS§164.945 164.947 165A.310 et seq.
LA				X	12§201 et seq.

State		Agency	Requirements		Citation
ME	X	State Board of Education			20A§10701 et seq.
MD		State Board for Higher Education			§12-201 et seq. Education Code
MA		Board of Regents	X		69§30, 31
MI		State DOE	X		§390
MN		State Higher Education Coordinating Board			Chapter 136A, 61
MS		Commission on College Accreditation			§37-101-241
MO				X	§355.025
MT		Advisory Council	X		§20-30-101 et seq.
NE		Nebraska Coordinating Commission for Postsecondary Education	X		§79-2401 et seq.
NV		Commission on Postsecondary Education	Must be accredited by DOE or have its credits accepted by one DOE-accredited college		34§394.620 et seq. 34§394.383 et seq.
NH	Must be authorized by legislature	Postsecondary Education Commission			§292:8-b et seq.
NJ		Board of Higher Education			RSA 18A:68–1 et seq.
NM		Board of Education Finance	DOE + 3-letter rule, and any school with a "comparable" basic academic education		§21-23-3 et seq. Education Code
NY		DOE and University of the State of NY	DOE-accredited agency	X	16§216 et seq.
NC		Board of Governors			Chapter 116-15

Appendix A (continued)

	Agency	Accreditation	DOE-accredited agency		Citation
ND					§15-20.4-01 et seq.
OH	Board of Regents		X		§1713.01 et seq.
OK		Either Oklahoma State Regents for Higher Education or regional accreditation			70§4101 et seq.
OR	Oregon Educational Coordinating Comm.	Northwest Association of Schools and Colleges			§348.830 et seq.
PA	State Board of Higher Education				24§2421 et seq.
RI	Board of Regents				§16-40-1 et seq.
SC	State Commission on Higher Education	Institution accredited by a COPA agency	X		§59-46-10 et seq.
SD				X	§§ 47-22-1, -4
TN	Tennessee Higher Education Comm.		X		§49-7-2001
TX	Coordinating Board, Texas College and University System	X			§61.301 et seq. Ed. Code. Texas Codes Annotated
UT				X	§16-6-20 et seq.
VT	State Board				16§176
VA	State Council of Higher Education Regulatory Boards		X		Title 23, §§23-265 to 23-276
WA	Higher Education Coordinating Board	Accrediting agency recognized by state			§28B.85.010 et seq.
WV	West Virginia Board of Regents				§§18-26-13 18-26-13a

	Educational Approval Board	Accrediting agencies recognized by the Board; nonprofits	
WI			§38.51 §182.028
WY		X	§17-7-101

[a]A typical statute regulates higher or postsecondary education but excludes an accredited institution.
[b]Some of the standards refer to financial resources, faculty, facilities, courses of instruction, and student protection.
[c]All states require some type of license or charter. The states in this column, however, have only laws relating to nonprofit corporations.
[d]The Hawaii statute provides only that a college must state whether or not it is accredited.
Sources: State statutes effective as of April 1987.

REFERENCES

The Educational Resources Information Center (ERIC) Clearinghouse on Higher Education abstracts and indexes the current literature on higher education for inclusion in ERIC's data base and announcement in ERIC's monthly bibliographic journal, *Resources in Education* (RIE). Most of these publications are available through the ERIC Document Reproduction Service (EDRS). For publications cited in this bibliography that are available from EDRS, ordering number and price are included. Readers who wish to order a publication should write to the ERIC Document Reproduction Service, 3900 Wheeler Avenue, Alexandria, Virginia 22304. (Phone orders with VISA or MasterCard are taken at 800/227-ERIC or 703/823-0500.) When ordering, please specify the document (ED) number. Documents are available as noted in microfiche (MF) and paper copy (PC). Because prices are subject to change, it is advisable to check the latest issue of *Resources in Education* for current cost based on the number of pages in the publication.

Adams, A.V., et al. 1983. "The Neglected Source of Human Wealth: A Study of Formal Education and Training during the Adult Years." No. PB 83–153395. Springfield, Va.: National Technical Information Service. (Order from NTIS, 5285 Port Royal Road, Springfield, VA 22161.)

American Society for Training and Development. 1981. *Directory of Academic Programs in Training and Development/HRD.* Alexandria, Va.: Author.

———. 1986a. *ASTD Who's Who Membership Directory.* Alexandria, Va.: Author.

———. 1986b. *National Report on Human Resources.* Alexandria, Va.: Author.

Anderson, Richard E., and Kasl, Elizabeth Swain. 1982. *The Costs of Financing Adult Education and Training.* Lexington, Mass.: Lexington Books.

Andrews, Grover J. Winter 1979. "Assessing Nontraditional Education." *North Central Association Quarterly* 53(3): 336–57.

Andrews, Grover J., et al. 1978. *Assessing Nontraditional Education.* Washington, D.C.: Council on Postsecondary Education. ED 165 577. 222 pp. MF–$1.00; PC–$19.22.

Ashworth, Kenneth. 1979. *American Higher Education in Decline.* College Station: Texas A&M University Press.

Astin, Alexander. 1977. *Four Critical Years.* San Francisco: Jossey-Bass.

Babbidge, Homer D., Jr., and Rosensweig, Robert M. 1962. *The Federal Interest in Higher Education.* New York: McGraw-Hill.

Baker, Jeanette S. 1983. "An Analysis of Degree Programs Offered by Selected Industrial Corporations." Ph.D. dissertation, University of Arizona.

Becker, Gary. 1975. *Human Capital.* New York: Columbia University.

Ben-David, Joseph. 1972. *American Higher Education*. New York: McGraw-Hill.

Bender, Louis. 1983. "Accreditation: Misuses and Misconception." In *Understanding Accreditation*, edited by K. Young, C. Chambers, H.R. Kells, and associates. San Francisco: Jossey-Bass.

Bendix, Reinhard. 1956. *Work and Authority in Industry*. New York: John Wiley & Sons.

Blount, W. Frank. 1979. "The Corporate University: Training and Education in the Bell System." Testimony before the Senate Committee on Labor and Human Resources, 6–7 June.

Blumenfeld, Warren. 1966. "Attitude Change as a Criterion in Training." *Training and Development Journal* 20(9): 26–33.

Blumenfeld, Warren, and Crane, Donald P. 1973. "Of Training Effectiveness: How Good?" *Training and Development Journal* 27: 42–51.

Bowen, Howard R. 1977. *Investment in Learning*. San Francisco: Jossey-Bass.

Branscomb, Lewis M., and Gilmore, Paul C. Winter 1975. "Education in Private Industry." *Daedalus* 104: 222–33.

Brickman, William W., and Lehrer, Stanley. 1962. *A Century of Higher Education: Classical Citadel to Collegiate Colossus*. New York: Society for the Advancement of Education.

Brinkerhoff, Robert O. December 1981. "Making Evaluation More Useful." *Training and Development Journal* 35(12): 66–70.

Bronson, Walter G. 1914. *The History of Brown University, 1764–1914*. Providence, R.I.: Brown University Press.

Brubacher, John S., and Rudy, Willis. 1976. *Higher Education in Transition*. New York: Harper & Row.

Campbell, J.P.; Dunnette, M.D.; Lawler, E.E.; and Weick, K.E. 1970. *Managerial Behavior, Performance, and Effectiveness*. New York: McGraw-Hill.

Carnegie Council on Policy Studies in Higher Education. 1980. *Three Thousand Futures*. San Francisco: Jossey-Bass.

Carnevale, Anthony P. 1982. *Human Capital: A High-Yield Corporate Investment*. Washington, D.C.: American Society for Training and Development.

———. Jan. 1986. "The Learning Enterprise." *Training and Development Journal* 40: 18–26.

Carnevale, Anthony P., and Goldstein, Harold. 1983. *Employee Training: Its Changing Role and an Analysis of New Data*. Washington, D.C.: ASTD Press.

Chambers, Charles M. 1983. "Federal Government and Accreditation." In *Understanding Accreditation*, edited by K. Young, C. Chambers, H.R. Kells, and associates. San Francisco: Jossey-Bass.

Clarke, Robert G. 1984. "Customized Job Training and Credit Programs." In *Customized Job Training for Business and Industry*, edited by R.J. Kopecek and R.G. Clarke. New Directions for Community Colleges No. 4. San Francisco: Jossey-Bass.

Clark, Harold F., and Sloan, Harold. 1958. *Classrooms in the Factories*. Rutherford, N.J.: Fairleigh Dickinson University, Institute of Research.

Clement, Ronald W. Winter 1981. "Evaluating the Effectiveness of Management Training: Progress during the 1970s and Prospects for the 1980s." *Human Resource Management* 20: 8–13.

College Entrance Examination Board. 1984. *Training for Contract: College-Employer Profiles*. New York: Author.

Coordinating Board, Texas College and University System. 1980. "Allied Health Education in Texas: Guiding Concepts for the '80s." Coordinating Board Study Paper No. 29. Austin: Author. ED 191 418. 70 pp. MF–$1.00; PC–$7.29.

Council for Noncollegiate Continuing Education. 1985. *1985–86 Directory of Accredited Noncollegiate Continuing Education Programs*. Richmond, Va.: Author.

Council on Postsecondary Accreditation. 1981. "COPA: The Balance Wheel for Accreditation. A Guide to Interagency Cooperation." Washington, D.C.: Author.

———. 1986. *Council on Postsecondary Accreditation Self-Study*. Washington, D.C.: Author.

Craig, Robert L., ed. 1976. *Training and Development Handbook*. 2d ed. New York: McGraw-Hill.

Craig, Robert L., and Evers, Christine J. 1981. "Employers as Educators: The Shadow Educational System." In *Business and Higher Education: Toward New Alliances*, edited by G. Gold. New Directions for Experiential Learning No. 13. San Francisco: Jossey-Bass.

Cross, K. Patricia. 1981. "Partnerships with Business and the Professions." AAHE Current Issues in Higher Education No. 3. Washington, D.C.: American Association for Higher Education. ED 213 325. 27 pp. MF–$1.00; PC–$5.44.

Cross, K. Patricia, and McCartan, Anne-Marie. 1984. *Adult Learning: State Policies and Institutional Practices*. ASHE-ERIC Higher Education Report No. 1. Washington, D.C.: Association for the Study of Higher Education. ED 246 831. 162 pp. MF–$1.00; PC–$15.52.

Crowther, Samuel. 1923. *John H. Patterson: Pioneer in Industrial Welfare*. Garden City, N.Y.: Doubleday.

Davis, Eleanor. 1933. "Company Retraining Programs." Princeton, N.J.: Princeton University, Industrial Relations Section.

———. 1935. "Educational Refunds in Industry." Princeton, N.J.: Princeton University, Industrial Relations Section.

Davis, Howard, and Salasin, Susan E. 1975. "The Utilization of

Evaluation." In *Handbook of Evaluation Research*, edited by E.L. Struening and M. Guttentag. Beverly Hills, Cal.: Sage.

De L'Ain, Bertrand Girod. 1981. "Certifying Effect and Consumer Effect: Some Remarks on Strategies Employed by Higher Education Institutions." *Higher Education* 10(3): 55–73.

Dickey, Frank G., and Miller, Jerry W. 1972. *A Current Perspective on Accreditation*. AAHE-ERIC/Higher Education Report No. 7. Washington, D.C.: American Association for Higher Education. ED 068 071. 73 pp. MF–$1.00; PC–$7.29.

Douglas, Joel. 1984. "Do Academic/Corporate Partnerships Pose New Threats to Faculty Employment Relations in Institutions of Higher Education?" New York: National Center for the Study of Collective Bargaining in Higher Education and the Professions. ED 250 995. 8 pp. MF–$1.00; PC not available EDRS.

Dowling, John, and Pfeffer, Jeffrey. 1975. "Organizational Legitimacy, Social Values, and Organizational Behavior." *Pacific Sociological Review* 18(1): 122–36.

Dressel, P.L. 1976. *Handbook of Academic Evaluation: Assessment of Institutional Effectiveness, Student Progress, and Professional Performance for Decision Makers in Higher Education*. San Francisco: Jossey-Bass.

El-Khawas, Elaine. 1984. "Campus Trends." Higher Education Panel Report No. 65. Washington, D.C.: American Council on Education. ED 252 171. 29 pp. MF–$1.00; PC–$5.44.

Eurich, Nell P. 1985. *Corporate Classrooms: The Learning Business*. Carnegie Foundation for the Advancement of Teaching. Lawrenceville, N.J.: Princeton University Press.

Flamholtz, Eric. 1974. *Human Resource Accounting*. Encino, Cal.: Dickenson Publishing Co.

Gilbert, Thomas. November 1976. "Training: The $100 Billion Opportunity." *Training and Development Journal* 30: 3–8.

Glidden, Robert. 1983. "Specialized Accreditation." In *Understanding Accreditation*, edited by K. Young, C. Chambers, H.R. Kells, and associates. San Francisco: Jossey-Bass.

Goldstein, Harold. 1980. *Training and Evaluation by Industry*. Washington D.C.: National Institute for Work and Learning.

———. 1982. "Using Data on Employee Training from the Survey of Participation in Adult Education (Current Population Survey)." *The Nature and Extent of Employee Training and Development: A State-of-the-Art Forum on Data Gathering*. Washington, D.C.: American Society for Training and Development.

Goodwin, R.C. 1950. *The Challenge*. Proceedings of the 4th Annual Conference of the Training within Industry Foundation, 24–26 May, Summit, New Jersey.

Green, Kenneth C. 1981. *Accreditation and Quality: Minimal*

Requirements versus Distinguishing Characteristics. New York: Exxon Education Foundation. ED 209 997. 29 pp. MF–$1.00; PC–$5.44.

Hader, John J., and Lindeman, Edward C. 1929. "What Do Workers Study?" New York: Workers Education Bureau.

Hamblin, Anthony C. 1974. *Evaluation and Control of Training.* London: McGraw-Hill.

Harcleroad, Fred F. 1980. *Accreditation: History, Process, and Problems.* AAHE-ERIC Higher Education Report No. 6. Washington, D.C.: American Association for Higher Education. ED 198 774. 60 pp. MF–$1.00; PC–$7.29.

Harcleroad, Fred F., and Dickey, Frank G. 1975. *Educational Auditing and Voluntary Institutional Accrediting.* AAHE-ERIC Higher Education Report No. 1. Washington, D.C.: American Association for Higher Education. ED 102 919. 45 pp. MF–$1.00; PC–$5.44.

Hawthorne, Elizabeth M. 1983. "Report on Preparation of HRD Professionals." Prepared for the Task Force on HRD/Workplace Education, Center for the Study of Higher Education, University of Michigan.

————. Forthcoming. *Evaluating Employee Training Programs: A Research-Based Guide for Human Resources Managers.* Westport, Conn.: Quorum Books.

Hawthorne, Elizabeth M.; Libby, Patricia A.; and Nash, Nancy S. 1983. "The Emergence of Corporate Colleges." *Journal of Continuing Higher Education* 31(2): 2–9.

Hickerson, Karl A., and Litchfield, Harry E., III. 1978. "Professionalism vs. Salesmanship: Focusing on Evaluation Procedure at John Deere." *Training and Development Journal* 32(4): 53–59.

Hodgkinson, Harold L. 1981. "Impact of National Issues." In *Improving Academic Management,* edited by P. Jedamus and M. Peterson. San Francisco: Jossey-Bass.

Hofstadter, Richard, and Hardy, C. DeWitt. 1952. *The Development and Scope of Higher Education in the United States.* New York: Columbia University Press.

Hofstadter, Richard, and Smith, Wilson, eds. 1961. *American Higher Education: A Documentary History.* Vol. 1. Chicago: University of Chicago Press.

Hogarth, Robin M. 1979. *Evaluating Management Education.* New York: John Wiley & Sons.

Honan, James P. 1982. "Corporate Education: Threat or Opportunity?" *AAHE Bulletin* 34(7): 7–9. ED 214 453. 4 pp. MF–$1.00; PC–$3.59.

International Association of Universities. 1970. "Methods of Establishing Equivalencies between Degrees and Diplomas." Paris: UNESCO.

Johnson, Eldon. 1981. "Misconceptions about the Early Land-Grant Colleges." *Journal of Higher Education* 52(4): 333–42.

Jones, J.A.G. 1971. "Toward a Cost-Benefit Approach to Evaluating Management Training." Paper read at IPM National Conference, England.

Kane, Michael J. 1941. "Training Programs for Supervisors and Employees." Address and discussion before the Eleventh Annual Conference on Industrial Relations. 17–18 April, University of Michigan.

Kaplin, William A. 1975. *Respective Roles of Federal Government, State Governments, and Private Accrediting Agencies in the Governance of Postsecondary Education.* Washington, D.C.: Council on Postsecondary Accreditation. ED 112 816. 39 pp. MF–$1.00; PC–$5.44.

Kearsley, Greg. Summer 1977. "The Cost of CAI: A Matter of Assumptions." *AEDS Journal* 10: 100–12.

———. 1982. *Costs, Benefits, and Productivity in Training Systems.* Reading, Mass.: Addison-Wesley.

Keeton, Morris T., ed. 1980. *Defining and Assuring Quality in Experiential Learning.* New Directions for Experiential Learning No. 9. San Francisco: Jossey-Bass.

Kells, H.R., and Parrish, Richard. 1979. "Multiple Accrediting Relationships of Postsecondary Institutions in the United States." COPA Technical Report No. 1. Washington, D.C.: Council on Postsecondary Accreditation. ED 175 359. 63 pp. MF–$1.00; PC–$7.29.

Kelly, Roy Willmarth. October 1919. "Employment Management and Industrial Training." Bulletin No. 48, Employment Management Series No. 4. Washington, D.C.: Federal Board for Vocational Education.

Kirkpatrick, Donald L. 1967. "Evaluation of Training." In *Training and Development Handbook*, edited by R. Craig. New York: McGraw-Hill.

———. June 1979. "Techniques for Evaluating Programs." *Training and Development Journal* 33: 78–93.

Kirkwood, Robert. 1978. "Student Mobility and Transfer." In *Credentialing Educational Accomplishment*, edited by J. Miller and O. Mills. Washington, D.C.: American Council on Education.

Kopecek, Robert J., and Clarke, Robert G. 1984. *Customized Job Training for Business and Industry.* New Directions for Community Colleges No. 4. San Francisco: Jossey-Bass.

Lawrence, Judith, and Green, Kenneth. 1980. *A Question of Quality: The Higher Education Ratings Game.* AAHE-ERIC Higher Education Report No. 5. Washington, D.C.: American Association for Higher Education. ED 192 667. 76 pp. MF–$1.00; PC–$9.56.

Likert, Rensis. 1961. *New Patterns of Management*. New York: McGraw-Hill.

Lusterman, Seymour. 1977. *Education in Industry*. New York: The Conference Board.

———. 1985. *Trends in Corporate Education*. Report No. 870. New York: The Conference Board. ED 195 636. 108 pp. MF–$1.00; PC–$11.41.

Luther, David B. 1984. "Partnerships for Employee Training: Implications for Business and Industry." In *Customized Job Training for Business and Industry*, edited by R.J. Kopecek and R.G. Clarke. New Directions for Community Colleges No. 4. San Francisco: Jossey-Bass.

Lynton, Ernest A. no date. *The Role of Colleges and Universities in Corporate Education*. Boston: Center for Studies in Policy and the Public Interest.

———. 1981. "Colleges, Universities, and Corporate Training." In *Business and Higher Education: Toward New Alliances*, edited by G. Gold. New Directions for Experiential Learning No. 13. San Francisco: Jossey-Bass.

———. 1984. *The Missing Connection between Business and the Universities*. New York: American Council on Education/Macmillan Publishing Co.

McGarraghy, John J., and Reilly, Kevin P. 1981. "College Credit for Corporate Training." In *Business and Higher Education: Toward New Alliances*, edited by G. Gold. New Directions for Experiential Learning No. 13. San Francisco: Jossey-Bass.

McGehee, William, and Thayer, Paul. 1961. *Training in Business and Industry*. New York: John Wiley & Sons.

McGuire, W. Gary. 1984. "Worker Education for Improved Productivity: The Role of New York State Community College Contract Courses." In *Customized Job Training for Business and Industry*, edited by R.J. Kopecek and R.G. Clarke. San Francisco: Jossey-Bass.

McQuigg, Beverly. 1980. "The Role of Education in Industry." *Phi Delta Kappan* 61(5): 324–25.

Maeroff, Gene. 13 August 1981. "Business Is Cutting into the Market: Becomes Competitor for Colleges Looking to Adult Enrollees." *Survey of Continuing Education. New York Times*.

Mahler, Walter R. 1976. "Executive Development." In *Training and Development Handbook*, 2d ed., edited by R.L. Craig. New York: McGraw-Hill.

Main, Jeremy. 11 January 1982. "Why Engineering Deans Worry a Lot." *Fortune*.

Mant, Alistair. 1977. *The Rise and Fall of the British Manager*. New York: Holmes & Meier.

Mayville, William V. 1972. *A Matter of Degree: The Setting for Contemporary Master's Programs*. AAHE-ERIC Higher Education Report No. 9. Washington, D.C.: American Association for Higher Education. ED 071 623. 51 pp. MF–$1.00; PC–$7.29.

Miner, Mary G. 1977. *Management Training and Development Programs*. No. 116. Washington, D.C.: Bureau of National Affairs.

———. 1978. *Training Programs and Tuition Aid Plans*. No. 123. Washington, D.C.: Bureau of National Affairs.

Morse, Suzanne. 1984. *Employee Educational Programs: Implications for Industry and Higher Education*. ASHE-ERIC Higher Education Report No. 7. Washington, D.C.: Association for the Study of Higher Education. ED 258 501. 99 pp. MF–$1.00; PC–$9.56.

Mortimer, Kenneth P. 1984. *Investment in Learning: Realizing the Potential of American Higher Education*. Report of the Study Group on the Conditions of Excellence in Higher Education. Washington, D.C.: National Institute of Education.

National Center for Education Statistics. 1984. *Digest of Education Statistics, 1983–1984*. Washington, D.C.: Author. ED 244 402. 238 pp. MF–$1.00; PC–$21.49.

Office of Personnel Management. October 1979. *The Participant Action Plan Approach: An Introduction*. Washington, D.C.: Office of Personnel Management, Workforce Effectiveness and Development.

Office of Technology Assessment. 1982. "Information Technology and Its Impact on American Education." Washington, D.C.: U.S. Government Printing Office.

Olson, Lawrence. 1986. "Training Trends: The Corporate View." *Training and Development Journal* 40(9): 32–35.

Orlans, Harold. 1975. *Private Accreditation and Public Eligibility*. Lexington, Mass.: Lexington Books.

O'Toole, James. 1978. *Work, Learning, and the American Future*. San Francisco: Jossey-Bass.

Parrish, Richard. 1980. "A Study of the Relationships between Eligibility for Licensing in Various Professions and Accreditation for the States of Delaware, Maryland, New Jersey, and Pennsylvania." ED 197 700. 52 pp. MF–$1.00; PC–$7.29.

Peckham, Howard H. 1967. *The Making of the University of Michigan, 1817–1967*. Ann Arbor: University of Michigan Press.

Peterfreund, Stanley. May 1976. "Education in Industry: Today and in the Future." *Training and Development Journal* 30: 30–40.

Peterson, Dorothy G. 1979. "Accrediting Standards and Guidelines." Washington, D.C.: Council on Postsecondary Accreditation. ED 172 708. 176 pp. MF–$1.00; PC–$17.37.

Pitre, Lee Frances. 1980. "Credit and Noncredit Education Opportunities Offered by Large Industrial Corporations." Ph.D. dissertation, University of Texas at Austin.

Quackenboss, Thomas C. April 1969. "White-Collar Training Takes Many Forms." *Training and Development Journal* 23: 16–26.

Regents of the University of the State of New York, Program of Noncollegiate-Sponsored Instruction. 1977. "Follow-through Study." Albany: University of the State of New York.

————. 1983. *A Guide to Educational Programs in Noncollegiate Organizations.* Albany: University of the State of New York. ED 195 798. 353 pp. MF–$1.00; PC–$29.30.

Rittenhouse, Sandra S.; Breitler, Alan; and Phillips, R. Garland. 1980. *NET: Needs Assessment and Evaluation of Training.* Washington, D.C.: Office of Personnel Management, Office of Productivity.

Rudolph, Frederick. 1962. *The American College and University: A History.* New York: Vintage Books.

Salinger, Ruth and Barlett, Joan. Spring 1983. "Evaluating the Impact of Training: A Collection of Federal Agency Evaluation Practices." No. PB 83–261149. Springfield, Va.: National Technical Information Service. (Order from NTIS, 5285 Port Royal Road, Springfield, VA 22161.)

Salinger, Ruth and Roberts, C. Spring 1984. "Evaluating the Impact of Training: A Collection of Federal Agency Evaluation Practices." No. PB 84–179464. Springfield, Va.: National Technical Information Service. (Order from NTIS, 5285 Port Royal Road, Springfield, VA 22161.)

Schultz, Theodore W. 1971. *Investment in Human Capital: The Role of Education and of Research.* New York: Free Press.

Shellum, Bernie. 13 December 1981. "GMI Engineers: A Future without GM." *Detroit Free Press.*

Sorge, Marjorie. 10 March 1986. "UAW, GM Create Joint 'U'." *Detroit News.*

Southern Association of Colleges and Schools. 14 December 1977. "Standards of the College Delegate Assembly." Atlanta: Author.

Sproul, Lee S. 1981. "Beliefs in Organizations." In *Handbook of Organizational Design: Adapting Organizations to Their Environments,* edited by P.C. Nystrom and W.H. Starbuck. Oxford: Oxford University Press.

Spurr, Stephen H. 1970. *Academic Degree Structures: Innovative Approaches.* New York: McGraw-Hill.

Steinmetz, Cloyd S. 1976. "The History of Training." In *Training and Development Handbook,* 2d ed., edited by R.L. Craig. New York: McGraw-Hill.

Stevens, John A. 1977. "Academic Gatekeepers: State Responsibilities in Granting Degree Authority. The Case at Massachusetts General Hospital." Mimeographed. Cambridge, Mass.: Harvard University.

Stufflebeam, Daniel L. 1974. *Evaluation in Education: Current Applications*. Berkeley: McCutchan Publishing.

Taylor, Frederick Winslow. 1967. *The Principles of Scientific Management*. New York: W.W. Norton & Co.

"Training within Industry." mimeo, undated.

Training within Industry Foundation. 1950. Proceedings of the 4th Annual Conference, 24–26 May, Summit, New Jersey.

U.S. House of Representatives, Committee on Education and Labor/ U.S. Senate, Committee on Labor and Public Welfare. 1975. *A Compilation of Federal Laws, as Amended through December 31, 1974, Prepared for the Use of the . . . Committees*. Washington, D.C.: U.S. Government Printing Office.

Veysey, Lawrence R. 1965. *The Emergency of the American University*. Chicago: University of Chicago Press.

Vroom, V.H. 1964. *Work and Motivation*. New York: John Wiley & Sons.

Weaver, David Andrew, ed. 1949. *Builders of American Universities*. Vol. 1. Alton, Ill.: Shurtleff College Press.

Weeks, David A., ed. 1975. *Human Resources: Toward Rational Policy Planning*. Conference Board Report No. 669. New York: The Conference Board.

Wells, S. 1977. "Cost Analysis of Televised Instruction for Continuing Professional Education." *Instructional Science* 5(2): 259–82.

Woodward, Nicholas. 1975. "The Economic Evaluation of Supervisor Training." *Journal of European Training* 4(3): 134–47.

Yarmolinsky, Adam. April 1976. "Challenges to Legitimacy: Dilemmas and Directions." *Change*: 18–25.

Young, Kenneth E. 1983. "Prologue: The Changing Scope of Accreditation." In *Understanding Accreditation*, edited by K. Young, C. Chambers, H.R. Kells, and associates. San Francisco: Jossey-Bass.

Young, Kenneth, and Chambers, Charles. 1980. "Accrediting Agency Approaches to Academic Program Evaluation." In *Academic Program Evaluation*, edited by E.C. Craven. New Directions for Institutional Research No. 27. San Francisco: Jossey-Bass.

Young, Kenneth; Chambers, Charles; Kells, H.R., and associates. 1983. *Understanding Accreditation*. San Francisco: Jossey-Bass.

Zemke, R. 1983. "U.S. Training Census and Trends Report, 1982–83." Minneapolis: Lakewood Publications.

INDEX

A

Academic freedom, 61, 73
Academic recognition, 29, 61, 69–70
Accreditation
    approaches, 61–62
    definition, 43–44
    importance, 79–80
    issues, 54–56, 59, 69
    public trust, 80
    specialized, 37, 61
    voluntary, 22, 47–48
Accrediting agencies
    approaches, 60–63
    control issue, 55–56
    formal recognizers, 70–72
    types, 43, 44, 48, 49
ACE (see American Council on Education)
Admission criteria, 39
Advanced Management Program (Harvard), 28
Age factor
    participation, 7
    work force, 65
Agriculture resource courses, 11
Allied health professions, 22
American Association of Bible Colleges, 43
American Council on Education (ACE), 29, 44, 49, 51, 52,
    69, 70, 73, 75
American Dietetics Association, 44
American Institute of Banking, 21, 36
American Management Association, 25, 26, 54
American Society for Training and Development (ASTD),
    26, 28
American Society of Training Directors, 26
Angell, James B., 30
Apprenticeships, 25
Architecture courses, 20
Arthur D. Little Management Education Institute, 21, 22, 36
Arts and sciences, 38
Associate degrees, 1, 21, 82
Association of American Law Schools, 44
ASTD (see American Society for Training and Development)
AT&T, 5, 6, 53

B

Baccalaureate degrees, 20, 35, 72
Banking, 21

Formal Recognition of Employer-Sponsored Instruction   105

Basic adult education, 11
Bell and Howell, 20
Bell Labs, 13
Bishop Clarkson College of Nursing, 36, 37
Blue collar workers, 26
Boston Architectural Center, 20, 37, 61
Brown University, 31
Business courses, 11, 38

C
California State Bar, 37
Carnegie-Mellon University, 82
Case studies, 85
Centennial Exposition of 1876, 35
Certificate programs, 21
Certification, 44, 81
CETA job training program, 21
Chartering process, 56
Chrysler Institute of Engineering, 21
CIBAR Systems Institute, 21
CNCE (see Council for Noncollegiate Continuing Education)
College of Health Sciences, 36
College of Insurance, 36, 37
Colorado: cooperative programs, 21
Communication skills courses, 11
Community colleges, 75, 77
Company size factor, 6
Competitive edge, 77
Computer science (see also Software engineering), 38, 82
Consortia, 22
Construction employees, 6
Continuing education, 9, 70
Cooperative programs, 22, 38–39, 41–42, 51, 80–82
COPA (see Council on Postsecondary Accreditation)
Cornell University, 31
Corporate colleges
        definition, 2, 15
        degree-granting characteristic, 20
        development examples, 20–22
        flexibility, 39
        founding rationale, 35–38
        justification, 54
        list, 16–19
        mission, 61
Corporate education
        centers, 67, 81

Formal recognizers
    corporate education, 79–80
    postsecondary education, 70–74
For-profit corporate colleges, 20
Franklin Institute, 31
French language courses, 82
Functional-technical education, 11, 75, 83

G

General Electric, 28, 54
General Motors, 36, 38, 58, 82
General Motors Institute, 22, 36, 38, 58, 61
G.I. Bill, 32
Governance, 40, 55, 57–58, 60
Government regulation, 45–48
Graduate education, 22, 31
Graduates: corporate vs. traditional, 83

H

Harvard College, 29, 30, 86
Harvard University, 28
Higher education (traditional)
    adaptability, 78
    corporate college comparison, 38–40
    dissatisfaction, 66–68
    education for employment, 86
    exchange of credits, 72
    graduates, 83
    joint ventures, 81–82
    perceived noncooperation, 41–42
    pricing policies, 78
    procedural slowness, 68
    recipients, 80
    scheduling inflexibility, 67
    state agencies, 73–74
Hoe and Company, 25
Honeywell, 54
Hospitals, 36
Hughes Aircraft, 29

I

IBM, 82
Illinois: regulation, 21, 51
Independent board of directors, 60
Industrial needs, 35

Line managers as trainers, 10
Little, Arthur D., 36

M
Management education, 10–12, 21, 27, 28, 38
Managerial employees, 6, 7, 8
Manufacturing employees, 6
Marjorie Webster Junior College v. *Middle States Association of Colleges and Secondary Schools*, 56, 58, 80
Massachusetts
    Board of Higher Education, 57, 58, 73
    Board of Regents, 57
    degree-granting authority, 39, 45
    regulation, 51, 60
Massachusetts General Hospital, 57, 58
Massachusetts Institute of Technology (MIT), 6, 82
Master's degrees, 21, 22, 35, 36, 38, 54
Middle managers, 7
Middle States Association of Colleges and Schools, 37, 56, 80
Midwest Industrial Management Association, 21–22
Minimum competencies, 72
Mission, 34–39
Missouri: degree-granting authority, 21
Morrill Acts of 1862 and 1890, 31
Motorola, 82

N
National Architectural Accrediting Board, 37
National Association of Corporate Schools, 25, 26
National Association of Schools of Art and Design, 80
National Association of Schools of Music, 45
National Association of Trade and Technical Schools, 48
National Cash Register Company, 25
National Center on Research on Postsecondary Teaching and Learning, 84
National College of Education, 28
National Educational Corporation (NEC), 20
National Industrial Conference Board, 28
National League of Nursing, 48, 71
National Registry of Credit Recommendation (ACE), 49, 51
National Society of Sales Training Executives, 26
National Technological University, 22
National Training Incentives Act, 53
NCR, Inc., 12, 25
NCR Management College, 13
NEC (see National Educational Corporation)

New England Association of Schools and Colleges, 57, 80
New York
 Board of Regents, 29, 44, 49, 51, 52, 69, 70, 73, 75
 regulation, 51
Nonmanagement employees, 8
Nonprofit corporate colleges, 20
Nontraditional education, 54–55
North Central Association of Colleges and Schools, 37, 48
Northeastern Illinois University, 28
Northrop Aeronautical Institute, 35
Northrop Corporation, 35
Northrop Institute of Technology, 35
Northrop University, 21, 35, 36, 37, 38
Norton Company, 82
Nursing, 22, 36, 71

O
On-the-job training, 5, 8, 84
Organizational change, 84
Organizational structure, 13–14, 85
Orientation courses, 11
Outcomes evaluation, 14–15, 54–55
Owl College, 12

P
Participation levels, 6–8
Part-time programs, 39, 67
Patterson, John H., 25
Personal services courses, 11
Personnel promotion, 66
Petroleum Industry Training Directors, 26
Philadelphia College of Textiles and Science, 35, 36, 37,
 38, 39
Postdoctoral fellowships, 38
Princeton University, 28, 30
Private colleges similarity, 59–60
Private Industry Councils, 52
Productivity, 15
Professional associations
 corporate college formation, 21
 industrial trainers, 26
 meetings, 7
Professional education, 31
Professional employees, 6, 8
Program recognition, 48–49
Proprietary institutions, 20, 21, 85

Public utilities employees, 6
Purchase of educational enterprise, 20
Puritan tradition, 29

Q
Quality
      control, 69, 71
      curriculum, 59–62
      finance, 58
      governance, 57–58

R
Rand Graduate Institute of Policy Studies, 22
Rationale, 35–38
Recognition
      approaches, 56–63
      corporate motivation, 52–54
      courses, 49
      current status, 50–51
      formal, 45–48, 70–74
      individuals, 49–50
      informal, 50
      institutional, 48
      interest in, 3
      program, 48–49
      research on, 86
Relevance, 39
Remedial education, 10, 11, 77
Research opportunities, 83–87
Retraining, 8
Rio Salado Community College, 82

S
St. Lawrence University, 36
Sales personnel, 8, 25, 26
Scheduling, 39, 67
Seagate Center, 67
Search, Theodore, 35
"Shadow educational system," 2
Skill building, 77
Smith-Hughes Act of 1971, 26
Software engineering, 21, 22, 36, 38, 39
Spending levels, 5–6
Standards, 48, 49, 62, 71, 72

State action
        degree-granting authority, 73
        higher education agencies, 73–74
        laws, 89–93
        regulation, 45, 47, 50, 51, 59–60, 69–70
        standards, 48, 49
        statutes (chart), 46
Students
        ability to work in groups, 68
        characteristics, 84
        financial aid, 47
        part-time, 85, 86
Supervisors, 6, 7
Swain School of Design, 80

T
Tappan, Henry Phillip, 30
Tax advantages, 53
Teaching methods, 12–13, 38–39
Technical employees, 6, 7, 8
Technology, 65
Tenure, 40
Texas Instruments, 13, 29
Textile courses, 20
Trade Adjustment Assistance Extension and Reform Act, 53
Trade associations
        corporate college formation, 21
        meetings, 7
Trade employees, 6
Trainers: preparation, 10
Training vs. education, 1, 67
Training within Industry, 27
Training within Industry Foundation, 28
Transfer credit, 44
Transportation employees, 6
Trends
        collegiate education, 29–32, 65–68
        delivery systems, 28–29
        noncollegiate education, 40–42
Tuition reimbursement, 8, 9, 82
1202 commissions, 73

U
Union College, 30
United Auto Workers, 82
University of Michigan, 30, 84

University of Pennsylvania, 30
University of Toledo, 67
University of Virginia, 30
University seminars, 8
University System of New Hampshire, 82
U.S. Department of Education approval, 47, 48, 56
U.S. Military Academy, 30

V

Vestibule schools, 12, 25
Virginia: recognition of individuals, 49
Vocational Education Acts of 1946, 26
Vocational schools, 20

W

Wang, An, 22, 36, 39
Wang Institute of Graduate Studies, 21, 22, 36, 38, 39
Wang Laboratories, 36
Wayland, Francis, 31
Western College Association, 35
Westinghouse Electric Robotics Institution, 82
White, Andrew D., 31
White collar workers, 7
Wilson, Woodrow, 32
Woodward, Augustus, 30
Worcester State College, 82
World War II, 26–27, 32, 35, 49

X

Xerox Corp., 13, 53

Y

Yale Report of 1828, 31

ASHE-ERIC HIGHER EDUCATION REPORTS

Since 1983, the Association for the Study of Higher Education (ASHE) and the ERIC Clearinghouse on Higher Education at the George Washington University have cosponsored the ASHE-ERIC Higher Education Report series. The 1987 series is the sixteenth overall, with the American Association for Higher Education having served as cosponsor before 1983.

Each monograph is the definitive analysis of a tough higher education problem, based on a thorough research of pertinent literature and institutional experiences. After topics are identified by a national survey, noted practitioners and scholars write the reports, with experts reviewing each manuscript before publication.

Eight monographs (10 monographs before 1985) in the ASHE-ERIC Higher Education Report series are published each year, available individually or by subscription. Subscription to eight issues is $60 regular; $50 for members of AERA, AAHE, and AIR; $40 for members of ASHE (add $7.50 for postage outside the United States).

Prices for single copies, including 4th class postage and handling, are $10.00 regular and $7.50 for members of AERA, AAHE, AIR, and ASHE ($7.50 regular and $6.00 for members for 1983 and 1984 reports, $6.50 regular and $5.00 for members for reports published before 1983). If faster 1st class postage is desired for U.S. and Canadian orders, add $.75 for each publication ordered; overseas, add $4.50. For VISA and MasterCard payments, include card number, expiration date, and signature. Orders under $25 must be prepaid. Bulk discounts are available on orders of 15 or more reports (not applicable to subscriptions). Order from the Publications Department, ASHE-ERIC Higher Education Reports, the George Washington University, One Dupont Circle, Suite 630, Washington, D.C. 20036-1183, or phone us at 202/296-2597. Write for a publication list of all the Higher Education Reports available.

1987 ASHE-ERIC Higher Education Reports

1. Incentive Early Retirement Programs for Faculty: Innovative Responses to a Changing Environment
   Jay L. Chronister and Thomas R. Kepple, Jr.

2. Working Effectively with Trustees: Building Cooperative Campus Leadership
   Barbara E. Taylor

3. Formal Recognition of Employer-Sponsored Instruction: Conflict and Collegiality in Postsecondary Education
   Nancy S. Nash and Elizabeth M. Hawthorne

1986 ASHE-ERIC Higher Education Reports

1. Post-tenure Faculty Evaluation: Threat or Opportunity?
   Christine M. Licata

2. Blue Ribbon Commissions and Higher Education: Changing Academe from the Outside
   Janet R. Johnson and Laurence R. Marcus

3. Responsive Professional Education: Balancing Outcomes and Opportunities
   Joan S. Stark, Malcolm A. Lowther, and Bonnie M.K. Hagerty

4. Increasing Students' Learning: A Faculty Guide to Reducing Stress among Students
   Neal A. Whitman, David C. Spendlove, and Claire H. Clark

5. Student Financial Aid and Women: Equity Dilemma?
   Mary Moran

6. The Master's Degree: Tradition, Diversity, Innovation
   Judith S. Glazer

7. The College, the Constitution, and the Consumer Student: Implications for Policy and Practice
   Robert M. Hendrickson and Annette Gibbs

8. Selecting College and University Personnel: The Quest and the Questions
   Richard A. Kaplowitz

1985 ASHE-ERIC Higher Education Reports

1. Flexibility in Academic Staffing: Effective Policies and Practices
   Kenneth P. Mortimer, Marque Bagshaw, and Andrew T. Masland

2. Associations in Action: The Washington, D.C., Higher Education Community
   Harland G. Bloland

3. And on the Seventh Day: Faculty Consulting and Supplemental Income
   Carol M. Boyer and Darrell R. Lewis

4. Faculty Research Performance: Lessons from the Sciences and Social Sciences
   John W. Creswell

5. Academic Program Reviews: Institutional Approaches, Expectations, and Controversies
   Clifton F. Conrad and Richard F. Wilson

6. Students in Urban Settings: Achieving the Baccalaureate Degree
   Richard C. Richardson, Jr., and Louis W. Bender

7. Serving More Than Students: A Critical Need for College Student Personnel Services
   Peter H. Garland

8. Faculty Participation in Decision Making: Necessity or Luxury?
   Carol E. Floyd

1984 ASHE-ERIC Higher Education Reports

1. Adult Learning: State Policies and Institutional Practices
   K. Patricia Cross and Anne-Marie McCartan

2. Student Stress: Effects and Solutions
   Neal A. Whitman, David C. Spendlove, and Claire H. Clark

3. Part-time Faculty: Higher Education at a Crossroads
   Judith M. Gappa

4. Sex Discrimination Law in Higher Education: The Lessons of the Past Decade
   J. Ralph Lindgren, Patti T. Ota, Perry A. Zirkel, and Nan Van Gieson

5. Faculty Freedoms and Institutional Accountability: Interactions and Conflicts
   Steven G. Olswang and Barbara A. Lee

6. The High-Technology Connection: Academic/Industrial Cooperation for Economic Growth
   Lynn G. Johnson

7. Employee Educational Programs: Implications for Industry and Higher Education
   Suzanne W. Morse

8. Academic Libraries: The Changing Knowledge Centers of Colleges and Universities
   Barbara B. Moran

9. Futures Research and the Strategic Planning Process: Implications for Higher Education
   James L. Morrison, William L. Renfro, and Wayne I. Boucher

10. Faculty Workload: Research, Theory, and Interpretation
    Harold E. Yuker

1983 ASHE-ERIC Higher Education Reports

1. The Path to Excellence: Quality Assurance in Higher Education
   Laurence R. Marcus, Anita O. Leone, and Edward D. Goldberg

2. Faculty Recruitment, Retention, and Fair Employment: Obligations and Opportunities
   John S. Waggaman

3. Meeting the Challenges: Developing Faculty Careers
   Michael C.T. Brookes and Katherine L. German

4. Raising Academic Standards: A Guide to Learning Improvement
   Ruth Talbott Keimig

5. Serving Learners at a Distance: A Guide to Program Practices
   Charles E. Feasley

6. Competence, Admissions, and Articulation: Returning to the Basics in Higher Education
   Jean L. Preer

7. Public Service in Higher Education: Practices and Priorities
   Patricia H. Crosson

8. Academic Employment and Retrenchment: Judicial Review and Administrative Action
   Robert M. Hendrickson and Barbara A. Lee

9. Burnout: The New Academic Disease*
   Winifred Albizu Meléndez and Rafael M. de Guzmán

10. Academic Workplace: New Demands, Heightened Tensions
    Ann E. Austin and Zelda F. Gamson

*Out-of-print. Available through EDRS.

NOTES

NOTES

NOTES